2 way street

DISCOVERING THE

REWARDS OF MENTORING

Erika Forbes & David Kupfer

2WAYSTREETMENTORING.com

2 Way Street: Discovering the Rewards of Mentoring

Library of Congress Preassigned Control Number 2021902967

ISBN 978-0-9993061-2-3

Printed in the United States of America

Published by Meadows Communications LLC

Edited by Louisa Williams

Designed by Todd Germann

Table of Contents

Introduction

Who needs a mentor?

This is a good question, but we pose a better, bigger one:

Who *doesn't* need a mentor?

Mentoring is not a new concept or practice. The word goes back at least to the ancient Greeks. Its historical context includes early medical research, in which mentoring by doctors led to notable early discoveries in understanding and treating human illness.

Then and now, mentoring represents a form of teaching, but also a form of abstract guidance. It borrows elements from apprenticeship, coaching, advising, sponsorship, counseling, and even parenting.

Traditionally, mentoring has meant that a more experienced, higher-ranking person provides a less experienced, lower-ranking, younger person with education, guidance, and modeling for career or life. In many institutions, mentoring lasts a few years and ends when the junior colleague gets promoted or moves away.

We emphasize our perspective using the metaphor of a two-way street, with both mentor and mentee contributing and learning. Using lessons learned in our own academic lives and in our work in an institute dedicated to launching careers in mental health research, in this book we offer an expanded philosophy of mentoring, one we believe is especially well suited to the scholars, researchers, and teachers who work in today's diverse, rapidly changing world.

In recent years mentoring has become popular in the corporate arena, but it has always been an essential element of academic culture. In academia, work and training could not happen without mentoring. Medical researchers learn by adopting techniques, contributing to research, and analyzing and writing up data from their mentors' labs, while scholars of literature learn through reading and evaluating primary and critical texts with their mentors. Scholarly content aside, academics in all fields often learn from their more experienced colleagues how to navigate the university system, advance through the ranks, and improve critical skills such as negotiating. Effective mentoring ultimately prepares the mentee to become a mentor. In this way, mentoring sustains and perpetuates excellence in a field.

Today's academic realities make mentoring especially valuable. Choosing a career path, obtaining funding, finding a faculty position, moving to a new institution, and dealing with unprofessional behavior are just some of the many challenges that an effective mentor can help a young scholar navigate. Mentoring provides help for early-stage academics who are finding their way in this competitive and sometimes lonely setting, offering opportunities for developing technical skills, networking, and learning from someone who has experienced both failure and triumph. But we have also seen that mentoring is crucial at every stage of a career, as scholars and teachers progress through the ranks, accept new jobs and challenges, become mentors to others, consider changing focus, and even look to retirement.

Why are we writing another book about mentoring?

Corporate mentoring guides abound, but no book that we're aware of addresses the specialized needs of mentors and mentees in today's society. And the mentoring books written to date define mentors as seasoned veterans and mentees as inexperienced professionals, two individuals who meet face-to-face in their university or institution, discuss career matters, and then part company when the younger person moves on or up.

Our view is much wider. We see mentoring as an experience that contributes to lifelong career and character development for both people involved. Effective mentoring, we have learned, can happen across time zones and even international borders, connecting individuals in different institutions and even different fields at different career stages. Some mentoring relationships last a short time, and others stretch for years and change with the career paths of both participants. Mentoring isn't necessarily an exclusive arrangement, either: people often benefit from having several mentors at any one time. Wherever and however good mentoring happens, it's always a two-way street, an opportunity for both mentor and mentee to learn and grow.

We believe that like all valuable skills and practices, mentoring should be studied, analyzed, taught, and practiced with care and attention. In today's academic world, mentoring takes place across university departments, in professional organizations, and at meetings from the local to the international. But before people sign on to receive mentoring or serve as mentors in academic settings or professional associations, shouldn't they know exactly what mentoring is and how to do it well? What is expected of mentors? Of mentees? What works? What is the role of appropriate behavior? Diversity, equity, and inclusion? Or technology? This book is our answer to those questions.

Who we are

We are professors of psychiatry who have worked for many years at the University of Pittsburgh. David Kupfer's work has included long-term treatment strategies for recurrent mood disorders, the pathogenesis of depression, and the relationship between biomarkers and depression. Erika Forbes's research addresses the development, pathophysiology, and treatment of depression from a neuroscience perspective, focusing on adolescent mental health and the role of the brain's emotional and reward systems. We are also directors, along with Alan Schatzberg, professor of psychiatry at Stanford University, of the Career Development Institute for Psychiatry (CDI, www.cdi.pitt.edu), which is co-located at the University of Pittsburgh and Stanford University in Palo Alto, California.

The goal of the CDI is to help junior-level scientists launch their careers in mental health research, with a focus on the critical skills that are key to success but aren't a part of one's scientific training.

The CDI is a formal program based on a model of scientific training developed by David during his 26 years as chair of the Department of Psychiatry at Pitt, one that focuses on collaboration, negotiation, funding, and growth, all through mentoring and a supportive department culture. At Pitt, these principles are instantiated through a weekly seminar for postdoctoral fellows in psychiatry, whether they hold PhDs, MDs, or other doctoral degrees. This approach has led to a farm-team system of sorts, in which many faculty members who arrived at Pitt as psychiatry residents, clinical psychology interns, or postdoctoral fellows have stayed for decades. The CDI's goal is to make this model available to a larger, national pool of talented young scientists.

Many departments, programs, or institutions for young scientists follow a different model. Perhaps they don't plan to retain the junior scientists who've trained there, or perhaps they follow a strict apprenticeship model in which a trainee works directly with one mentor and doesn't receive guidance from other mentors or from the department. The National Institute of Mental Health, however, took note of Pittsburgh's success in retaining junior scientists. Along with Alan, who was then chair of the Department of Psychiatry and Behavioral Sciences at Stanford University, David obtained funding from NIH to establish the CDI in 2003. This began the adventure that has provided mentoring for more than 200 scientists.

In our own careers and in the CDI, we've observed mentoring from several vantage points. We've been mentees of mentors, mentors of mentees, mentors of mentors, and facilitators of mentor-mentee relationships. In many ways, the CDI, which Erika joined in 2006 and became a director of in 2015, has been our laboratory, an opportunity to test mentoring approaches and formulate a philosophy of mentorship as well as practical guidelines for implementing that philosophy. This book describes our philosophy and practices in a format we hope will be accessible to individual scholars, research groups, departments, and institutions.

How will this book help?

Throughout these pages we provide present-day examples of mentoring challenges. We cover both sides of this dyadic relationship, and we look at how mentoring can be effective at various career stages. We tackle myths about mentoring and help you understand how identity and ways of dealing with others influence the mentoring experiences for both mentor and mentee. Through exercises, we aim to help you assess where you are today, as someone giving or receiving mentoring, and how you can improve. We also share lessons we've learned from the CDI.

We wrote this book with seven goals in mind:

1 | Include conceptual and practical issues

We don't just want to promote a model of mentoring. We want to make mentoring more effective and rewarding through direct help for those involved in it.

2 | Address both mentors and mentees

These two groups aren't typically the audience for the same book, but each can benefit from understanding the other's perspective and challenges. Knowing that many mentees will not learn all they need to know from their own mentors, we aim to provide the tools and skills for mentees to become effective mentors, to help them help others—and find satisfaction in the process.

3 | Provide information based on today's academic culture

Technology has created new opportunities and challenges, and mentoring now takes many forms, from peer mentoring groups to short-term dyadic mentoring to speed mentoring.

4 | Emphasize interpersonal issues

Effective mentoring requires trust and respect. To invest in someone else's career progress—or to accept that investment—requires strong interpersonal skills and healthy self-awareness. This book identifies these skills, examines how they can be learned, and suggests what to do when someone is not a good mentor or crosses an ethical boundary.

5 | Address appropriate and inappropriate behavior

Problem behaviors can poison the mentor-mentee relationship. Except in peer mentoring, an imbalance of power is part of every mentor-mentee relationship, so we focus on ensuring that both mentors and mentees understand and practice ethical behavior.

6 | Emphasize the value of diversity, equity, and inclusion

In today's workplaces, women and mentees from under-represented groups still face many challenges. Good mentors should be aware of this reality, be open to learning from their mentees, and help mentees deal with discrimination or any unwelcoming behavior.

7 | Provide tools for improvement

Each chapter includes background information, vignettes based on composites from our own or our colleagues' experience, and tips for mentors and mentees. Most chapters end with an exercise.

The book's language and structure

In today's work culture, there is increasing awareness—for good reason, we say—of the ways that power can be misused to hurt people who are early in their careers. When we use the word "status" in this book, we aren't referring to anyone's value as a human being. Instead, we're thinking of a socially constructed, workplace-defined position in an institutional hierarchy, one that can confer power and privilege to some and vulnerability to others.

A few other terms deserve explanation. Throughout the book we use the nongendered pronoun "they" and employ "LGBTQ+" to refer to all the sexual orientation and gender identity communities in the academic and mentoring world, while recognizing that each group has different experiences. "Academia" is our term for large, research-focused universities, scholarly institutes, small liberal arts colleges, and any other institution where higher education or research takes place.

Section 1 of this book covers the basics, including our mentoring philosophy, definitions, and the qualities and skills that are essential for mentoring.

Section 2 takes things a step further to address sophisticated skills, difficulties that often arise, and the multiple versions of mentoring that exist today.

Section 3 addresses critical topics in workplace culture that inherently promote strong mentoring: diversity and inclusiveness, professional behavior, and technology.

Please join us on this journey. We hope that you will gain skills and broaden your perspective, and we think you might be surprised by what you already know as well as what you haven't yet considered. And we think you'll have fun.

CHAPTER 1
What is Mentoring?

In our professional lives, we started out with traditional views of mentoring, but our approaches have evolved to encompass a range of behaviors, formats, and experiences that are much wider than we first expected.

Here's our current-day definition: Mentoring is a professional relationship in which one person instructs, guides, inspires, supports, and encourages the other. The mechanics and timing of their exchanges might vary, but the mentor's and mentee's focus is always on the career success of the less experienced person. It can also be an opportunity for the mentor to learn new skills and see ideas and approaches to problems in a new light. When mentoring works well, information, interest, and insight all flow back and forth.

Our three principles of mentoring

1 | Mentoring is an essential professional experience. It leads to faster career progress, greater work satisfaction, and a stronger professional network. In academia, it promotes scholarly achievement.

2 | Mentoring is built on empathy and flexibility. Effective mentors and mentees adapt to each other's temperament, work styles, and behavior, shifting goals as the mentee progresses. Mutual caring and concern make the relationship work.

3 | Mentoring can be learned and should be taught. Anyone with basic professional qualifications and good interpersonal skills can learn to be a strong mentor. That said, mentoring isn't for everyone. If you don't enjoy mentoring, think of it as an obligation, or aren't interested in honing your skills, you should hope you aren't compelled to do it. If you are interested in learning or perfecting your skills, keep reading.

Case Example 1 | Effective Mentoring in a Nontraditional Setting

Leslie, a postdoctoral fellow, meets with her mentor Alan every other week for 45 minutes. She sets an agenda ahead of time and asks for his guidance on plans or decisions and his feedback on written projects. They have established a routine, with a regular schedule and clear expectations, meeting to check in and assess progress even when no deadline looms. Alan, a former department chair at a prestigious university who is now a busy researcher and consultant, is an expert on a new treatment technique that is rarely used in research. He has been generous about helping Leslie broaden her professional network, recommending she contact other experts when he thinks she could use their advice. Leslie recently started a study using the technique Alan specializes in, and the chance to get his expert opinion has been welcome.

Leslie and Alan are deliberate about their work together. They set goals for Leslie's work every six months and use the time between to assess her progress toward earlier goals. Alan enjoys trying to figure out what Leslie needs, and several of his creative suggestions have propelled her career progress.

Leslie and Alan's relationship has many of the characteristics of successful mentoring, but it's nontraditional. Because they are affiliated with different universities in different parts of the country, Leslie and Alan meet primarily through videoconference, although they make an effort to get together in person at scientific conferences. Leslie has a primary mentor at her own university who's the sponsor of her funding, knows how helpful Alan has been, and welcomes his involvement.

Case Example 2 | **A Long View of Mentoring**

Ellen has known Holly for 12 years, ever since Holly served on Ellen's dissertation committee. Ellen went on to become a postdoctoral fellow in Holly's lab, where Holly helped Ellen learn conceptual and empirical approaches, choose a research theme, conduct a study addressing the theme, forge collaborations, obtain a large-scale research grant, and get her first faculty position.

Although Ellen and Holly now work at different universities, the two have stayed in touch. Ellen, now an associate professor, still considers Holly a mentor, and Holly serves as an expert consultant on two of Ellen's current studies. Ellen has made her own reputation, and her niche in the field has made her a valuable collaborator for Holly.

Both Ellen and Holly are respected scientists with impressive accomplishments, and what was once an early-stage mentoring relationship has evolved into a collaboration. Moreover, they have developed a friendship, know each other's families, and spend time talking about personal as well as professional topics. They ask each other's advice and often plan studies as peers.

As these examples illustrate, mentoring need not be restricted to one location or one mentor, can be a long-term endeavor, and can change with circumstances. Alan and Leslie have a productive and satisfying mentoring relationship even though they work in different settings and meet in person only occasionally. Alan is Leslie's secondary mentor, providing perspective and expertise that complement those of her mentor at her own university. Ellen and Holly are no longer in the early, formal stages of mentoring but have maintained their relationship, changing it to suit their needs. They're proof that mentoring can last a long time and include many roles, from teacher to advocate to sponsor to friend.

What does mentoring look like? The traditional view vs. our view

	TRADITIONAL VIEW	OUR VIEW
Developmental Phase	■ Early in the mentee's career (e.g., during postdoctoral fellowship)	■ Lifelong ■ Any phase of career development
Content	■ Theoretical and practical aspects of the mentor's academic area	■ Scholarly tools, career issues, and life skills ■ General skills such as negotiating
Location	■ Same institution ■ Same department ■ In the same lab or suite	■ Anywhere in the world ■ Similar or different academic field
Academic Level	■ Higher-ranking, older mentor ■ Lower-ranking, younger mentee	■ A range of possible career or institutional levels, from equals (as in peer mentoring) to widely disparate ■ Mentor could be older, younger, or same age as mentee ■ Difference evolves as both members advance in their careers

	TRADITIONAL VIEW	OUR VIEW
Style	■ Mentor takes a uniform approach to all mentees	■ Mentor understands each mentee's strengths and challenges ■ Mentor provides what's needed for each mentee ■ Mentor appreciates the influence of identity, gender, and culture
Number of Mentors	■ One mentor : one mentee	■ As many mentors as needed ■ A mentoring team is an option
Frequency of Interactions	■ Weekly or biweekly ■ On a fixed schedule	■ Over days, weeks, or months ■ Ranges from regularly scheduled to as needed ■ Can include a single interaction, as in speed or conference mentoring
Setting	■ In person	■ Also by video conference, phone, text, social media direct message
Agenda	■ Set by mentor	■ Set collaboratively ■ Determined by setting mentee's goals, evaluating progress, and identifying challenges
Professional network	■ Mentor and mentee are insulated from larger community	■ Mentor introduces mentee to their network ■ Both broaden their networks
Direction of influence	■ Mentor to mentee	■ Bidirectional ■ The relationship is an alliance and a collaboration
Negotiation skills	■ Not taught or applied	■ Taught and practiced explicitly and directly ■ Part of the relationship

About mentors and mentees

What are the functions and responsibilities of a mentor? Except in peer mentoring (a topic we cover in Chapter 6), the mentor has more professional experience and higher status than the mentee, a fact that puts certain responsibilities onto the mentor's shoulders.

Being an effective mentor is a tall order, but it's one that can be broken down into manageable parts, each of which can be learned (or taught) and improved with practice. Good mentors teach, sharing knowledge, expertise, and resources; provide guidance for scholarly and career development; understand each mentee's unique qualities and adapt to them; focus on the mentee's goals rather than exclusively on the mentor's own goals; help mentees determine what will be most helpful; and evaluate their own progress and seek to improve.

Being a good mentee involves a little less responsibility but just as much focus and attention. Mentees who want to get the most out of their experience understand that fame and success alone don't make someone a good mentor; choose mentors who will be committed to the mentee's success and have relevant expertise and resources; and set clear goals. Those who benefit most also ask for help from mentors when needed; consider creating a team of mentors who can assist with various challenges at various times; evaluate progress; and always think of ways to improve.

Some mentoring fundamentals

To make all this happen, both mentor and mentee should:

Be self-aware, understanding their own and each other's strengths and shortcomings. The mentor should be clear about their motivations and skills for mentoring. The mentee should know—or be able to figure out—what they want from the arrangement.

Have a clear philosophy of mentoring—and communicate it. This is primarily the mentor's job, but if both people involved understand the parameters and goals of their work, their time together will be much more efficient and productive.

Set a tone and respect it. The mentee bears some responsibility for making the arrangement work, of course, but especially at the start, the mentor will probably have to frame the relationship by setting a constructive, professional tone and clearly identifying ground rules, goals, deadlines, expectations, and work styles.

Be realistic about the time, energy, and resources required to make the relationship work well. For both people involved, this means budgeting time for face-to-face or video meetings and reviewing material. But for the mentor, it also can mean being available on short notice, advocating in other arenas, and helping during difficult decision times.

Adapt to the other person's needs and work style. And adapt again as things change. As the more established professional, the mentor is responsible for getting to know each mentee, focusing on how that person communicates and what will help the mentee succeed. Change is part of every career trajectory, and both mentor and mentee should recognize when adjustments are needed. Mentees will have to make decisions about research projects, expand into new areas of expertise, and even abandon scholarly paths that are no longer fruitful. For a mentor, helping with these requires knowing where the field is going, appreciating the mentee's own strengths and preferences, and taking a dynamic view of academic work.

Remember that failure is part of success. Michael Jordan, whom many consider the greatest basketball player in history, has famously described failure as central to his accomplishments. "I've missed more than 9,000 shots in my career," he said in a script for a Nike commercial. "I've lost almost 300 games. Twenty-six times, I've been trusted to take the game-winning shot and missed. I've failed over and over and over again in my life. And that is why I succeed." As every experienced academic knows, failure is more common than success, and developing a thick skin—or at least accepting the inevitability of rejection—is an important survival skill. Mentors should make sure mentees learn how not to be derailed by setbacks.

Focus on the importance of saying no. Successful people in any field know how to protect their time, stay focused on their activities, and avoid making promises they can't keep. This isn't always easy, especially for young academics from under-represented groups, many of whom will be asked to serve on committees and projects where diversity is a concern. One approach is to develop phrases that are useful when a quick and diplomatic response is needed. These should include an acknowledgment of the request, a clear "no," and some kind of apology, but they don't always require a concrete reason.

Scripts for saying no

- Thanks for the invitation, but unfortunately, I have to decline.

- It's against my policy to take on new projects during the next six months. (This one is nice because people rarely argue with someone's "policy.")

- I've reached the limit for the number of [reviews, chapters, meetings] that I can complete effectively at once, so I won't be able to do this one.

- I've thought carefully about this, and I regret that I won't be able to say yes. Is there another way I could contribute?

- I'm honored by the request, but it turns out that I won't be able to be involved. I'll be happy to suggest other colleagues who have appropriate expertise. (This follows the etiquette for reviewing, in which just saying no isn't enough.)

Other aspects of mentoring: networking, sponsorship, and advocacy

Mentoring needn't be restricted to a dyad. The mentor should broaden the mentee's professional network by introducing the mentee to key leaders in the field, people who could become collaborators or mentors. This gives the mentee visibility, forges contacts with other researchers whose work is relevant, and helps the mentee understand the purpose, advantages, and challenges of building a professional network.

Sponsorship and advocacy will develop naturally from a successful mentoring relationship. Effective mentors who recognize potential will go out of their way to talk about a mentee to colleagues, nominate the mentee for prizes, and include the mentee in professional organizations and meetings. Advocacy can also mean being a spokesperson or protector: if a mentee needs help addressing a challenge or contacting someone outside the mentee's circle, a good mentor will take the mentee's side, represent the mentee's interests, and even, when appropriate, speak on the mentee's behalf.

It's not just networking and it's also not role modeling

Simply introducing a mentee to colleagues with high standing or significant resources won't help the mentee succeed. What will help is getting to know the mentee's strengths and potential and connecting the mentee with others who will appreciate those talents and provide opportunities.

Mentoring is distinct from role modeling. All of us, especially young people, can learn powerful lessons about setting goals, making professional choices, being public scholars, and managing competing demands by observing others. Role models might be close colleagues, friends, public figures, or others who catch our attention. They can guide and inspire, but they're not mentors who commit to someone's success and work closely with them to help make it happen. Still, role models can play a critical role in young academics' development, especially for women and those from under-represented groups. Just seeing someone who is "like you" and successful in the field can have a powerful influence, especially if the young person has frequent opportunities to observe how the role model manages the many challenges of academic life.

 ## Myths about mentoring

People often hold outdated views of how and when mentoring occurs. Here are some of the most harmful we've heard.

- **A scholar, researcher, or teacher can thrive without it.**
  Some mentees see mentoring as an obstacle to their success. If the mentor would just get out of their way, they think, they could accomplish more and achieve faster. There are lone wolves in any field, but the collaborative, multi-disciplinary nature of academia today often demands collective effort. Mentors can assist mentees in practical ways, but they're especially helpful in connecting mentees to the social networks they'll need to collaborate, obtain big opportunities, and build their reputations. A good mentor will always know when it's time to get out of the mentee's way.

- **If mentoring has to happen, get it over with.**
  In this view, being a mentor is another entry in a busy academic's to-do list. For the mentee, mentoring is a necessary evil, just another part of paying dues. The best mentoring relationships, however, are anything but an obligation. They're connections that make careers and lives much more enjoyable.

- **The ideal mentor is high-ranking, powerful, and famous.**
  Someone might impress friends and colleagues by having a mentor who's accomplished, well-known, and powerful. But commitment and interest are much more important than rank and resources alone.

■ **A mentor must work in the mentee's area of expertise.**
When trying to learn a technique or topic, a mentee should certainly choose someone in that area. But because good mentors are much more than teachers, mentees should consider whether someone's expertise—in academic culture or grant-writing, for example—can cross disciplines and provide a fresh perspective.

■ **Mentors are useful only at the early-career level.**
Mentoring can be critical after someone's first years, when a mentee on the verge of independence needs support, guidance, and advice. It can also be helpful for more established faculty members as they chart new stages in a long career, make decisions about scholarly topics, and consider big changes.

■ **A good mentor can work well with any mentee.**
Someone who works well with one mentee or at one career stage might not be a great fit for others or even for the same mentee at another time.

■ **A mentor and a mentee are stuck with each other.**
Mentors and mentees can find that their personalities, work styles, or goals aren't harmonious. But as in any tough situation, there are always options.

■ **The mentee should become a mini-me of the mentor.**
A good mentor guides but doesn't prescribe and appreciates that each mentee could eventually surpass the mentor. Success takes many forms.

■ **Mentoring is strictly a formal relationship.**
Mentoring can occur informally, in single or multiple contacts, and even without any explicit acknowledgment of mentoring. Helping others, giving advice, putting like-minded people in contact—sometimes mentors don't even know when they're mentoring. Staying in touch over years and careers, however, is one way to obtain flexible, valuable mentoring.

■ **Everyone should aspire to be a mentor.**
For various reasons, plenty of talented academics aren't suited to be mentors. That doesn't make them less accomplished or bad human beings. Ideally they can acknowledge this and proceed accordingly.

- **Mentoring is about the mentor's scholarly achievement.**
  In many academic settings, mentoring is not just a model for training people. It's the model for accomplishing work. Graduate students conduct research for their advisors under the guise of apprenticeship, and university faculty expect that their postdoctoral fellows will write papers to further the work in their labs. This can be good for all, but it can also create awkward situations. The self-serving model of mentoring is not one we admire or recommend.

- **Good mentors are born, not trained.**
  Some people take to mentoring more naturally than others, but anyone with some experience, interest, and an open mind can learn the skills of an effective mentor. And even the most successful, seasoned mentors can benefit from training and reflection.

Myths can be hard to dispel, but by remembering and practicing the basics of effective mentoring—empathy, understanding, and interest in others—we can create and benefit from modern-day models.

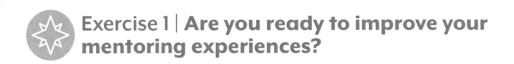

Exercise 1 | **Are you ready to improve your mentoring experiences?**

For Mentors

Check each item that fits your current mentoring experience or approach.

☐ I have developed a philosophy of how mentoring works.

☐ I adapt my mentoring to each mentee's needs.

☐ Mentoring contributes importantly to helping people succeed.

☐ I have the qualifications necessary for effective mentoring.

☐ When I want to improve my mentoring, I know how to find materials and resources.

☐ I know which aspects of mentoring—education, guidance, networking, coaching, advocacy—are natural for me and which are not.

☐ I feel enthusiastic about helping others make progress in their careers.

☐ I can balance my own career and scholarly goals with those of mentees.

☐ I have a good understanding of others' emotions, thoughts, and experiences.

☐ I know which mentees will be easier for me to work with and which will be more challenging.

☐ I know the common challenges for mentees in my field, and I'm prepared to help my mentees navigate them.

☐ I have tools for evaluating my mentees' progress and my effectiveness.

For Mentees

Check each item that fits your current mentoring experience or approach.

☐ I understand what is and isn't included in the mentoring relationship.

☐ My responsibilities as a mentee are clear to me.

☐ I can take steps to improve the quality of the mentoring I receive.

☐ I find it easy to be direct and clear with my mentor about my priorities.

☐ I can set up the logistical, practical structure of mentoring.

☐ I am able to work with more than one mentor.

☐ My criteria for selecting mentors include more than just rank and renown.

☐ I can identify my relative strengths and weaknesses for this career path.

☐ I am able to accept feedback and criticism.

☐ I know what drew me to this career and whether it will help me succeed.

☐ Setting boundaries and saying no are manageable for me.

☐ I know how to evaluate my progress.

CHAPTER 2
The Mentoring Relationship

The mentoring relationship has obvious basic elements and not-so-obvious nuances. At the very least, it is a professional dyad that lasts for a defined period and has concrete goals for the mentee's career development.

Our claim is that mentoring, practiced well and with continued care and attention, can be a long-term experience that ultimately leads to becoming colleagues. For this to happen, some fundamental elements should be clear early on and grow as time passes, the mentee's expertise increases, and the difference in rank between mentor and mentee diminishes.

This chapter is all about that evolving relationship, that dyad: how to set it up, how to deal with changing circumstances, how to handle setbacks, how to revisit and recommit when things aren't working well, and how to end up as partners who continue to help each other's careers.

We aim to offer recipes for success, but we also know that things don't always go smoothly—and that sometimes the best learning comes from observing or making mistakes.

Consider the following:

Case Example 3 | **Setting Ground Rules**

Jordan, a postdoctoral fellow, has worked with his primary mentor, Rachel, for almost a year, but the arrangement isn't going well. Jordan's main goals are to publish papers, get a grant from a foundation, and learn a technique that Rachel is famous for developing. But he has submitted only one paper, and he hasn't been able to meet with Rachel, who travels a lot, frequently enough to master the methods her lab uses. Rachel and Jordan get together only about once a month, and even then, Rachel often misses or is late for the meeting. Jordan had to send her four drafts of a recent paper before she returned it with edits.

Jordan feels far behind his peers, who seem more efficient at publishing their work and mastering methods, and he knows he needs to show progress soon. After talking with a professor and some peers, he develops a summary of his concerns and suggested solutions, practices it with friends, and finally presents it to Rachel face-to-face. He makes his promises and requests politely but clearly: he would like a specific meeting time each month, with an agenda he prepares; he will email written materials for Rachel's consideration at least three days before their meetings; he asks Rachel to tell him when he can expect her feedback; he wants a clear plan, with deadlines, to learn Rachel's clinical technique; and he would like to discuss his three main career goals at their next meeting.

Rachel has been frustrated with what she sees as Jordan's passivity, so she's taken aback by his list—and a little stunned to see her own tasks (and shortcomings) spelled out. But she credits Jordan for his honesty and initiative, tells him this, and agrees to negotiate a new set of expectations as he has suggested.

Case Example 4 | **Growing Pains in the Transition to New Roles**

Carolyn has been Sarah's mentor for four years, ever since Sarah moved to Carolyn's university to start her postdoctoral fellowship. Now an assistant professor, Sarah is feeling ready to shift to a more collaborative role with Carolyn. She's also been thinking about becoming a mentor herself. One step toward these new roles, she thinks, would be to become the senior author on papers, which in her academic area means being the last author listed.

Sarah has a paper in mind for this career milestone: a report by a trainee she's been supervising based on data from one of Carolyn's studies. But when Sarah asks Carolyn to edit what she thinks is a final version of the paper, complete with a list of authors, Carolyn doesn't answer for two weeks. Sarah sends Carolyn another draft, this time explicitly asking whether the order of authors is acceptable. Carolyn's reply doesn't mention the authors and instead raises questions that would require Sarah's trainee to re-analyze the data. Even after several email exchanges, the paper remains unsubmitted. Sarah eventually takes a direct approach: she tells Carolyn she wants to be senior author on this paper. Would Carolyn support that? Carolyn again evades the question and notes her own role as the principal investigator who received the funding and led the larger study on which the paper was based. Eventually, citing disagreement with one point in the paper, Carolyn tells Sarah that she doesn't want to be involved.

Once Sarah moves on to projects that don't involve Carolyn, Carolyn becomes friendly again. Sarah is relieved that she doesn't have to depend on Carolyn so completely for her career transition, and she is determined to maintain a productive, collegial mentor-mentee relationship. In time, the two are able to collaborate more explicitly and negotiate authorship more effectively.

Every relationship has rocky moments, and mentoring is no exception. For Jordan, Rachel, Carolyn, and Sarah, the big challenge is how to keep their relationships constructive and strong. Both Jordan and Rachel skipped over their basic early responsibilities: they never discussed Jordan's training needs, the frequency and contents of their meetings, how agendas would be set, how they would confer between meetings, and when materials and feedback would be exchanged. Sarah and Carolyn navigated those agreements early in their relationship, but things became strained when Sarah was ready for a new, less dependent role. Carolyn and Sarah never talked about the next phase of their mentoring—and what new expectations, policies, and plans it would present.

Both members of the dyad have a responsibility to make the mentoring relationship work. They contribute to the goals of mentoring in different but overlapping ways, as the following table describes.

How do key responsibilities further the goals of mentoring?

GOAL	MENTOR'S RESPONSIBILITY	MENTEE'S RESPONSIBILITY
Develop clear goals, plans, and expectations	■ Provide the structure for devising and recording goals, deadlines, terms of communication, and expectations ■ Revisit goals, rules, and expectations as needed	■ Be honest and realistic about goals and hopes ■ Be specific and clear about asking for help ■ If goals change, communicate this and be prepared to revise the mentoring agreement
Provide education and training for the mentee	■ Share expertise, techniques, career advice, and social networks ■ Provide timely and constructive feedback ■ Encourage the mentee to work with other mentors who have complementary skills and resources	■ Seek and accept feedback ■ Set meeting times, provide the mentor with materials for feedback in advance, and prepare agendas ■ Seek help from other mentors
Create a collaborative, respectful relationship	■ Provide a positive atmosphere for growth ■ Express encouragement, optimism, and confidence ■ Treat all mentees fairly and with respect, yet also with the individual attention they need (more about this in Chapter 5) ■ Use the wisdom of experience to guide the practical and interpersonal aspects of mentoring	■ In the spirit of behaviorism, which emphasizes reinforcement, provide praise and gratitude for effective, helpful, or timely behavior ■ Address issues of identity and background as they influence the mentoring relationship and career progress (see Chapter 7 for more)

Personal boundaries

Because everyone has individual preferences, strengths, and styles, each mentor-mentee relationship is different. Some are formal, while others might involve casual conversation as well as structured discussions. But whatever the tone and approach, each dyad needs to develop a relationship over time in which both mentor and mentee have the other's best interest at heart. Because this is a professional, not a personal, relationship, both partners must make efforts to keep behavior on the professional side of the line.

There are a couple of qualifiers here, of course. Mentoring relationships can certainly develop into personal relationships once the formal mentoring has ended or the mentee has risen to (or approaches) the mentor's rank. As in all relationships, however, the terms should always be mutual, with both parties generally being as formal or informal as the more reserved person prefers. A certain amount of discomfort is tolerable and perhaps even valuable for growth. If a mentee feels shy around a famous mentor, tolerating that feeling is probably a worthwhile tradeoff for training and guidance—and in the process, the mentee might learn how to relax in the company of accomplished colleagues. Any discomfort caused by unprofessional behavior, however, deserves immediate attention. (For more on that, see Chapter 8.)

Aside from this general advice, we believe that mentors and mentees face specific challenges when managing personal issues within the relationship.

Respect the boundaries of a professional, collegial, confidential relationship. The mentor can ensure that the relationship begins and continues in a professional way by not disclosing too much personal information, not asking personal favors of the mentee, and not asking the mentee to solve the mentor's own problems. If the mentor or mentee feels resentful or hurt by an action by the other, they must find a way to discuss it. Academic institutions can be small places where gossip flourishes, so both mentor and mentee should discuss confidentiality—what will remain private between the two? what will not?—early on. The mentee should understand and respect these boundaries, discussing and revisiting them when needed.

Remember that the mentor has advantages. Both members of the relationship deserve to be treated with respect and dignity. In the workplace, however, the mentor almost always has higher status and greater power—and therefore more responsibility for setting limits and offering consistent support and help. This can be challenging when a mentor is male and a mentee female, the mentor is from a privileged background and the mentee is from an under-represented group, or the mentor has higher social as well as professional status (more on this in Chapter 9). But acknowledging and understanding advantages is always important.

Respect individual preferences. Comfort levels depend on both participants' interpersonal styles and preferences, and only the two people involved know exactly what those are. One of our colleagues makes it a practice to take her research team out drinking to mark a special occasion or when the group is attending a conference. Others, knowing that some people prefer more formality or aren't comfortable around alcohol, might host dinners but never meet with mentees in bars. Some never spend time with mentees outside of work. Whatever people's preferences are, honoring them is every mentor's responsibility.

Help with personal matters. As mental health professionals, both of us have had trainees ask for help solving a personal problem such as depression following a difficult romantic breakup. We're very much in favor of self-care, and on these occasions we've been happy to provide mentees with referrals to crisis resources, employee assistance programs, or local therapists and to suggest practical actions such as requesting a deadline extension. When the inevitable human personal stressors occur—illness, loss of a friend or relative, financial problems, strain in personal relationships—a mentee and mentor should have ways to address them.

Academia can be a stressful place, especially for people who have mental health challenges or are otherwise vulnerable. One physics journal paper we can't forget, written by an early-career researcher, was dedicated to the memory of a colleague who committed suicide after experiencing difficulties with what the author called the "psychological brutality of the postdoctoral system." We urge anyone in a serious situation to to seek help—from a mentor, friends, family, and professionals.

Harmful agendas (hidden or overt)

Mentors and mentees should aim for the best kind of professional, mutually satisfying relationship—but also be aware of a few other possible scenarios. These challenging agendas, some of which might operate outside either person's awareness, can occur on both sides.

Mentors' selfish agendas

Building an empire

Some mentors like to accumulate a large stable of mentees to feel important and influential. But in that stable they're rarely able to give each mentee the careful, individual attention the mentee deserves. In choosing a mentor, a mentee should be wary of someone who could be overextended and unavailable.

Getting the mentor's work done

Doing the mentor's work is one way for a mentee to develop the expertise necessary for independence. But the mentee always deserves credit for work and some autonomy. There's a balance here: the mentor's goals are certainly important, but when apprenticeship becomes exploitation or career suppression, the mentee should consider leaving.

Meeting personal needs

There can be a dark side of mentoring, in which mentors ignore or violate professional, personal, and ethical boundaries. This basic betrayal of trust can entail abuse, exploitation, or neglect of mentees for the mentor's personal gain or satisfaction. (We address this issue in detail in Chapter 8.) Institutions are often all too slow to act on complaints about such inappropriate behavior.

Mentees' selfish agendas

Obtaining success by association

Some mentees believe that by simply being affiliated with someone successful, they'll become successful. Maybe they'll find the easy way around academic career-building (is there such a thing?) and become rock stars just by showing up. Maybe they'll gain the adoration of the leaders in their field without having to build their own network or create a name through their work. It just doesn't work that way.

Having someone else determine a career path

Many mentees experience confusion or ambivalence about their career goals, and others have clear goals but great difficulty meeting them. By listening, asking good questions, and suggesting options, mentors can clarify choices and help with decision-making, but the mentor should never be responsible for mapping out the mentee's larger career path.

How can mentees shape the mentoring relationship?

Mentees have more power than they might think. Even with the experience and status differences inherent in most mentoring relationships, every mentee can influence the quality of mentoring.

Here are some tips for mentees, partly inspired by Erika's Career Development Institute webinar titled "Managing Your Mentor."

■ **Figure out the mentor's style**

Does the mentor prefer to meet in the morning or afternoon, early or late in the week? To be reminded about deadlines and meetings several times? To get a lot of work done by email and reserve meetings for more complicated matters? Does the mentor tend to become distracted if meetings go on for more than 30 minutes? Learn about the mentor's work and mentoring styles and build on them.

■ **Communicate clearly and directly**

Ask questions, request advice, and let the mentor know what is and isn't effective. Express enthusiasm for work, and be clear about goals and challenges. Be clear about needs, whether this is a video meeting while the mentor is out of town or a detailed timeline for learning new methods. Ask for constructive criticism or evaluations of progress. If things aren't going as hoped, find a constructive way to discuss that, proposing solutions as well as identifying problems.

■ **Be transparent**

The mentoring relationship hinges on trust, and appropriate disclosure is part of creating and maintaining trust. If seeking additional mentorship, looking into other careers, or planning to move across the country, share this information with the mentor. A good mentor will be interested and supportive (and maybe not surprised).

■ **Behave professionally**

We devote more attention to this in Chapter 8, but take responsibility for one side of the relationship by speaking respectfully, regulating emotions, being aware of others' reactions, and keeping non-urgent personal issues private.

Sometimes, as we discuss in Chapter 9, generational differences can lead to behavior that can appear rude. Pay attention to workplace etiquette, which can vary from one institution to another and even among two departments (or two research groups) in the same place.

■ **Show gratitude**

Don't reserve thanks for times when guidance or collaboration has been spectacular. Acknowledge small but helpful steps, let the mentor know when things are working, and try to cultivate good vibes by fostering a friendly atmosphere, proposing new team projects, or suggesting improvements in work processes.

 How does the mentee individuate from the mentor?

In every mentoring relationship, especially those that span years, a mentee will eventually be ready to move on. The time for being sheltered by the mentor has ended, the chance to leave the proverbial nest has arrived, and at least one person in the relationship wants to redefine it. Like adolescence, when there's a push against parents, this stage in a mentee's career can involve negative emotions that create conflict but end up helping the separation process. The mentor needs to help the mentee achieve what ideally has been the goal all along: becoming an independent scholar.

The evolution from a formal relationship between people of different ranks to a partnership of peers almost always takes place over years, and it doesn't always happen in a linear, smooth way. But as time passes and trust and mutual benefit grow, boundaries become more fluid, and guidance and sharing—perhaps in the form of expertise or professional contacts—can flow in both directions. Mentors and mentees can end up as equal partners, peers, and even friends.

The mentoring relationship has some predictable challenges and stages, and the tips in this chapter should provide a strategy for creating a steady road. This road will be the basis for a productive journey toward the mentee's success.

Exercise 2 | Have you established the practical details of the mentor-mentee relationship?

We recommend planning around two aspects of mentoring: (1) the mentee's goals and (2) the mentoring process. Mentor and mentee should complete this exercise together at one of their first meetings, and then revisit it every six months.

Step 1: Setting goals

Focus on the most important plans for the next six months. Don't forget that mentoring involves tasks in several domains: training (mastering new techniques, learning conceptual material), productivity (publishing papers [in science fields] or books [in the humanities], obtaining funding, completing activities that will enhance your CV), and professional development (building a reputation, participating in professional meetings, broadening your network).

Make a plan, with details for each goal as follows:

■ **Identify the Goal**

■ **Determine the following:**

   ■ What is the Deadline?

   ■ What are the Mentor's Responsibilities?

   ■ What are the Mentee's Responsibilities?

   ■ What are the Steps toward This Goal?

Step 2: Setting terms and expectations

You can use this to frame your nuts-and-bolts conversation.

Practical Matters

- How often will you meet?
- How will you schedule meetings? Will you have a regular time?
- Will you always meet in person? Will you meet by email or video call as a backup?
- How will meetings be structured? Who will set the agenda? Who will run the meetings?
- Can the mentee drop by the mentor's office to talk?
- How far in advance will the mentee send materials for the mentor's review?
- How will the mentor and mentee set deadlines for important projects?
- What is the plan for authorship on projects conducted together?
- Who will own the data collected collaboratively?

Interpersonal matters

- What are your technology preferences for communication and interaction?
- How quickly will each of you return emails, texts, or phone calls?
- Will everything you address together be confidential unless specified otherwise?
- Are any topics off-limits?
- How will you respect each other's time at work, conferences, or department events?
- How will you know when this phase of the relationship is reaching a conclusion?

CHAPTER 3

What Makes an Effective Mentor?

Does good mentoring require skills you can learn or traits that you have from birth? Both, of course. Certain enduring temperamental qualities help, as do the interpersonal styles that usually go along with them. We all vary in the degree to which we're sociable or conscientious or irritable, and these facets help determine how we behave in mentoring relationships. Even those who find that good mentoring comes naturally, however, can always improve.

In this chapter, we examine the basic characteristics of effective mentors. If you're a mentor, we'll help you identify your strengths and challenges, understand the demands of mentoring, and figure out how to accommodate those demands. If you're a mentee, we'll help you focus on what's really important in choosing a mentor, beyond just reputation and expertise. If you can find a mentor with the ability to help you succeed, your journey will be much easier than it would be with someone who just can't deliver in important ways.

 Case Example 5 | **Too Much Control?**

Noah, an intern near the end of full-time clinical work in a psychiatry department, is looking forward to getting training in a treatment technique in a clinic run by his new supervisor, Meredith. Meredith is a few years into her position on the faculty of a major research university, and she is serious about becoming a good mentor. She says she wants to share her expertise with junior colleagues and watch them become productive scientists. One of a few local experts in this new treatment, she has made it known that she wants to help others learn it.

Noah spends several weeks studying the new technique, including sessions in which he observes Meredith working with patients. When the time comes for him to take the lead under Meredith's supervision, however, Meredith interrupts him when he speaks, corrects him in front of patients, and sometimes takes over the session. Noah feels humiliated and left out, but his main disappointment is that he isn't learning the treatment. After he discusses his experiences with others in his training program, several mentees back out of the rotation in Meredith's clinic.

Meredith is surprised and hurt by this. "I wanted to make sure that he was learning to conduct the treatment properly, and I was trying to model the correct behavior for him," she tells a colleague. "It was all part of my teaching style."

 ## Case Example 6 | **A Rock Star Mentor**

Dan's mentor is a superstar. With publications in top journals and a reputation for innovative work, Michael has a faculty position at a prestigious private university and seems to be someone who can provide Dan, a postdoctoral fellow, with opportunities to gain visibility and learn cutting-edge science. Michael, who has cultivated his reputation, has admirers all around the world. His lab has several large-scale studies underway and includes dozens of mentees and collaborators.

When Dan is preparing what he thinks is an important paper, he asks Michael for advice on where to submit it and which findings to include. To Dan's dismay, Michael replies that he wants to put Dan's paper on hold in favor of another, higher-priority paper that Michael says could bring more attention to the lab. He offers to make Dan a co-author and in return asks Dan to rerun several sets of data analyses for the paper and manage a team that is checking details.

Dan is at a pivotal point in his career: he is applying for faculty positions and needs to show other universities that he can publish in high-profile journals. Not wanting to offend Michael and telling himself that co-authoring a big paper will bring benefits, Dan agrees to put his own paper aside. The paper that Dan drops everything to work on, however, ends up in a second-tier journal and receives only a modest number of citations, and Dan finishes his two-year fellowship with far fewer publications than he'd hoped.

Mentors can hurt their mentees in several ways, including neglect, exploitation, excessive control, and self-centered demands. Meredith said she wanted to be an effective mentor, but for some reason (perhaps her focus on her own expertise and reputation?) she couldn't relax and let Noah take the primary role in the clinic. Michael, the superstar, was so caught up in his own goals that he could see Dan only as an assistant. What these two mentors lack is a genuine, caring interest in their mentees' strengths and plans, an ability to grant them autonomy, and a willingness to let them form their own identities.

In our view, a good mentor has a combination of qualities and qualifications that allow them to impart wisdom and guidance to mentees and the flexibility to change behavior as needed. But a mentor can't be successful without one essential characteristic: a genuine wish to help others make progress in their careers.

Respecting the importance of diversity is another crucial quality of effective mentors. In some ways, this is a natural extension of the core concept of adapting: if mentors strive to understand what each mentee needs for career development, in the process they'll notice mentees' identity-level differences such as race, gender, ethnicity, socioeconomic background, or LGBTQ+ identity. Mentors who care about diversity, equity, and inclusiveness are willing to address diversity directly with their mentees, even if this reaches beyond the mentors' own experience and comfort levels. They also try to understand their own biases and ask for feedback on their assumptions and behavior.

 Danger zones—and mismatches

The greatest potential danger to a mentee's ultimate success comes from a mismatch with a mentor's temperament or style or a mentor's difficulties in the social-affective domain. Temperament involves stable tendencies to experience and express emotions, behave in social contexts, follow rules, or embrace new experiences. The social-affective domain includes social norms such as cooperating with others and affective qualities such as regulating one's emotions and behaviors.

Personal qualities fall into three categories: interpersonal, intrapersonal, and professional.

Interpersonal qualities help someone understand the strengths, weaknesses, goals, needs, and struggles of other people. Intrapersonal qualities help a person understand and manage their own internal experiences. Professional qualities are those that allow someone to apply ethical principles and respond to the norms of their work culture.

Interpersonal

These characteristics include empathy, compassion, fairness, autonomy-granting, ability to inspire others, appreciation of others' goals, respect for individual differences, and general understanding of others' needs. A mentor who can't understand other people's experiences will have a difficult time providing the help that mentees need. When dealing with mentees, mentors need to have reserves of generosity, patience, and understanding, since a mentee typically wants to be self-sufficient but doesn't have the level of expertise that a mentor does. Ultimately, an effective mentor appreciates that the mentee is a separate person with a unique style, goals, and preferences. Valuing diversity and being aware of identity, experiences, and differences also require interpersonal understanding.

Intrapersonal

Effective mentors understand not just others but themselves. They have an awareness of their own strengths and limitations, knowledge of what they find rewarding or challenging, insight into their behavior, knowledge of their preferred interpersonal contexts, and awareness of their own thoughts and emotions. They can detect when their behaviors are interfering with the mentee's progress or the mentoring relationship, and they can take responsibility when they've crossed a line and owe an apology or amends.

Good mentors know and observe the rules of their cultures, institutions, and immediate work contexts. They have clear boundaries about how and when they interact with their mentees, they respect the people around them, and their behavior is guided by the belief that others have dignity. (We deal with this issue more extensively in Chapter 8.)

 Which roles do mentors play?

Some say that everyone needs mentors (likely more than one) to fulfill several roles. The coach provides strategy for getting work done, making career progress, and enhancing training. The star might be busy but can model the dazzling path toward success. The connector makes introductions to others, from potential collaborators to complementary mentors to future employers. The technician is a practical guide to the nuts and bolts of the mentee's work, such as lab techniques and institutional resources. Finally, the teammate is a mentor on a level similar to that of the mentee who understands the mentee's position, has similar goals, and is experiencing parallel challenges.

Maybe this is true, or maybe, as the cartoon on the next page shows, mentors can be classified into 9 different types, each with benefits and pitfalls.

National Institutes of...
THE NINE TYPES OF PRINCIPAL INVESTIGATORS

How to develop the key qualities of mentoring

Using Exercise 3 below, developed for a mentoring training program at the University of Wisconsin, a mentor can identify areas worth attention and track progress.

It's also helpful to look around and learn from others. Notice mentors in real life or in literature, film, and art. Observe people in non-work domains to see who's worth emulating (and who's not).

Here are some suggestions:

■ **Learn from mentor-mentee relationships and mentors in books, movies, and real life.**
The mentoring dyads of Ralph Waldo Emerson and Henry David Thoreau, Henry James and Edith Wharton, or Joyce Carol Oates and Jonathan Safran Foer are some examples from American literature. Mentor examples include Charlotte from E. B. White's novel *Charlotte's Web* (and films by the same name), Mary Poppins (in versions including books by P. L. Travers, films, or plays) and Yoda in the Star Wars franchise. There are many other famous mentors in the worlds of art, business, politics, and sports.

■ **Be self-aware about needs and goals and how they do—and don't—overlap with those of a mentee.**
Every human being has blind spots, wishes, and self-focused interests. Endeavor to become aware of these and keep them from interfering.

■ **Get feedback.**
We can't know how others perceive us or whether we're helpful unless we ask directly. This can often be uncomfortable, especially if the answers include what seem to be deficits. But it will be worth the effort.

If you were born with the traits, talents, and instincts that make you a great mentor, lucky you. But if you're like most of us, somewhat skilled but still on the learning curve, and you're intent on doing this work well, you'll get there.

Exercise 3 | For mentors: What's your mentoring competence?

Rate yourself on the following mentoring skills, using the 1-7 scale provided. Focus on your general skill level, not your level with any specific mentee.

< Not At All Skilled			Moderately Skilled			Extremely Skilled >	

Active listening

1	2	3	4	5	6	7	NA

Providing constructive feedback

1	2	3	4	5	6	7	NA

Establishing a relationship based on trust

1	2	3	4	5	6	7	NA

Identifying and accommodating different communication styles

1	2	3	4	5	6	7	NA

Employing strategies to improve communication with mentees

1	2	3	4	5	6	7	NA

Coordinating effectively with your mentees' other mentors

1	2	3	4	5	6	7	NA

Working with mentees to set clear expectations of the mentoring relationship

1	2	3	4	5	6	7	NA

Aligning your expectations with your mentees'

1	2	3	4	5	6	7	NA

Considering how personal and professional differences may impact expectations

1	2	3	4	5	6	7	NA

Working with mentees to set research goals

1	2	3	4	5	6	7	NA

Helping mentees develop strategies to meet goals

1	2	3	4	5	6	7	NA

Accurately estimating your mentees' level of scientific knowledge

1	2	3	4	5	6	7	NA

Accurately estimating your mentees' ability to conduct research

1	2	3	4	5	6	7	NA

Employing strategies to enhance your mentees' knowledge and abilities

1	2	3	4	5	6	7	NA

Motivating your mentees

1	2	3	4	5	6	7	NA

Building mentees' confidence

1	2	3	4	5	6	7	NA

Stimulating your mentees' creativity

1	2	3	4	5	6	7	NA

Acknowledging your mentees' professional contributions

1	2	3	4	5	6	7	NA

Negotiating a path to professional independence with your mentees

1	2	3	4	5	6	7	NA

Taking into account the biases and prejudices you bring
to the mentor/mentee relationship

1	2	3	4	5	6	7	NA

Working effectively with mentees whose personal background is different from your own
(age, race, gender, class, region, culture, religion, family composition, etc.)

1	2	3	4	5	6	7	NA

Helping your mentees network effectively

1	2	3	4	5	6	7	NA

Helping your mentees set career goals

1	2	3	4	5	6	7	NA

Helping your mentees balance work with their personal life

1	2	3	4	5	6	7	NA

Understanding your impact as a role model

1	2	3	4	5	6	7	NA

Helping your mentees acquire resources (e.g. grants, etc.)

1	2	3	4	5	6	7	NA

Available at https://uwmadison.col.qualtrics.com/jfe/form/SV_5jMT4fhemifK01n?Q_JFE=qdg
Reference: Fleming M, House S, Shewakramani Hanson V, Yu L, Garbutt J, McGee R, Kroenke K, Abedin Z, Rubio D.M. The mentoring competency assessment: Validation of new instrument to evaluate skills of research mentors. Acad Med. 2013;88(7):1002-1008.

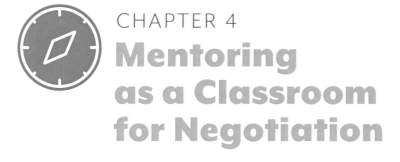

CHAPTER 4
Mentoring as a Classroom for Negotiation

Negotiating—trying to reach an agreement on a problem, challenge, or request of mutual interest—is a central part of mentoring. Oddly enough, many of the people who write about mentoring don't take much note of negotiation. Perhaps this is because they see it as an unnecessarily adversarial interaction or an activity outside the traditional academic skill set. But mentors and mentees negotiate with each other all the time, and mentoring is a context in which mentees can learn skills for negotiating effectively. Negotiation is not only a career enhancer but part of nearly every social interaction. Becoming an effective negotiator gives you a lifelong asset, so learning negotiating skills early—and constantly striving to improve them—just makes sense.

A negotiation is a collaboration. We negotiate to accomplish goals, whether that's authorship on a paper, better office space, a chance to work on a project, release from a responsibility, a salary for a new job, or a pay increase. Negotiating encompasses a variety of behaviors, including asking for what you want, saying no, trying to find mutual goals, presenting your position, and identifying options.

It involves interpersonal skills such as assertiveness as well as empathy and agreeableness. Negotiation skills are essential to functioning optimally as an academic—or as a human being—but are rarely taught in academic training.

For a broader discussion of negotiation in the context of academia, take a look at *Smart and Savvy: Negotiation Strategies in Academia*, written by David and his daughter Andrea Kupfer Schneider, a professor at Marquette University law school and an expert on negotiation and mediation. Here, however, we focus on the topic of negotiation as it's relevant to mentoring.

 ## Case Example 7 | **Resetting Priorities**

Carrie, an assistant professor, and her mentor, Rebecca, have had a productive three years. They've collaborated on peer-reviewed papers and grants, and Carrie's work with Rebecca has helped Carrie make a name for herself in the field. Now, however, Carrie is feeling pressure to boost her reputation and demonstrate her independence. She is finding it difficult to juggle her commitments: she has agreed to write two papers and a book chapter with Rebecca, but she also wants to start working toward the first papers from a study she conducted with a National Institute of Health-funded career development grant. Carrie feels that she has to choose between her work and Rebecca's writing projects.

After talking to some peers and thinking about her own and Rebecca's priorities, Carrie decides that she and Rebecca generally share the goal of publishing their work and that finishing all the projects, including her own, will be valuable for both of them. But because she thinks Rebecca is likely to feel slighted if Carrie seems to be changing her commitments, Carrie thinks carefully about how she'll make her case. She practices with a friend at work, trying to anticipate Rebecca's reactions and her own responses.

At their next weekly meeting, Carrie notes that while she enjoys writing with Rebecca and has committed to the three current projects, the question of how to balance those projects with her own work is creating a conundrum. She proposes a solution: she could shift responsibility for the book chapter to a colleague and postpone one of Rebecca's proposed papers but continue to work on the second collaboration paper as well as her own new paper. Rebecca, who is feeling behind in her own work, says she's not sure she can agree to postponing one paper. Carrie, expecting this concern, offers to remain involved in the book chapter in a smaller role and describes a timeline for each publication. Rebecca says she'll think about it. Carrie sends Rebecca a draft of the first paper before their next meeting, and when they're face-to-face, Rebecca thanks Carrie for sorting through the practical issues and agrees to Carrie's revised plan.

Case Example 8 | **Another Retention Package?**

Josh, a mid-career professor with a strong international reputation, is being courted by another university. After visiting the other school, meeting his potential colleagues, and outlining the resources he needs, he gets a job offer that includes a salary and details about facilities and funding. Now he needs to decide how to handle this with his department. The recruitment process started when the other department contacted Josh, and he entered the process with curiosity rather than a wish to leave his university, but he likes the new department. He also likes the idea of using this offer as leverage for a retention package, getting more money and resources at his current university. Josh wants to keep his plans private, so he decides not to consult his mentor, Mercedes.

Josh sets up a meeting with Amanda, his department chair, without saying what he wants to discuss, and tells Amanda about his job offer. Amanda (who has heard rumblings about Josh's visit to the other university) asks Josh how serious he is about leaving and notes that he has brought similar requests to her three times in the past five years. Although Amanda doesn't say this, Josh's new request annoys her, as she has put considerable effort and time into assembling past counteroffers, including conferring with her dean, who is reluctant to offer retention packages to any faculty member more than once every few years.

Josh makes a case for his value, emphasizing the other department's enthusiasm and generosity. But when Amanda doesn't mention a counteroffer, he gets flustered and doesn't follow through with his plan to request salary, research funding, or perks, and the meeting ends without a clear plan. When Josh checks in a week later, Amanda says only that she has considered the other offer, has talked to the dean, and will be in touch. Through one of her assistants, she later offers Josh a 5 percent raise. Surprised by what he views as a halfhearted attempt to keep him, Josh consults his mentor, Mercedes, who guesses that Amanda might not have the flexibility or motivation to propose more. Mercedes offers to talk to Amanda, and after that meeting explains the situation: their chair sees Josh as valuable to the department and hopes he'll stay, but she doesn't seem likely to reconsider. Josh ends up accepting the other university's offer, but he leaves wondering whether he painted himself into a corner.

Mentoring is an excellent framework in which people can practice the delicate dance of getting what they want while maintaining good relations with their dance partner. Saying no, as Carrie had to, is a skill that any researcher will need to perfect. If the relationship is a valuable one, a scholar or teacher will want to be able to resolve issues, understand goals, ask for things, and learn how to use empathy, flexibility, and understanding—of people and situations—to succeed. These are all essential parts of negotiation.

Carrie knows what she wants and can anticipate how Rebecca might react, but Josh, the young professor, is much less self-aware. Academics at many levels find themselves asking for resources, and having a job offer on the table can provide leverage. Josh, however, overestimated what his department chair, Amanda, could offer him and didn't consider the impact of his repeated requests for counteroffers—or how these might be viewed by Amanda or the dean. If he'd spoken to his mentor, Mercedes, earlier, he might have been able to see the situation through others' eyes.

Is negotiation really necessary?

Negotiating is essential to a successful career in academia. We're always balancing what we want, what other people want, and what circumstances dictate. We need resources, opportunities, and avenues for pursuing work. Others need the same, and sometimes we must find ways to make the best use of limited resources.

Finally, we all need to find ways to belong to communities (at best) or coexist with colleagues (at worst). If you learn how to negotiate early, your negotiation skills can mature along with your other career and academic skills.

Graduate students, medical residents, postdoctoral fellows, and assistant professors all need to make sure they have the resources and environment to launch their careers and their scholarly work. If mentors don't provide what mentees believe is essential to their success, mentees must learn to ask for what they need. Even if mentors do provide what's essential, oversight, disagreement, or changes in needs or resources will be inevitable. Either way, mentees need to learn how to get what they need.

 Negotiating skills probably aren't part of your usual curriculum

Academics are at a big disadvantage when it comes to negotiating. Other professions, such as business or law, openly acknowledge the value of negotiating and encourage people to learn it early in their careers. Unfortunately, in our world, this subject is largely ignored.

Why is negotiation a taboo topic in academia? Are scholars and teachers and researchers uncomfortable acknowledging that things don't always go smoothly? Is this part of the idea that academics are pursuing vocations, not careers, and that they're pure enough of heart to assume that everything is fair and appropriate? Whatever the explanation, we believe that if they don't directly help their mentees learn this essential skill, mentors are failing.

Mentees usually learn about negotiation by observing their mentors' behavior. Since some mentors are better negotiators than others, this is not an ideal way to learn, but determining what you do and don't admire about your mentor's negotiating style and skills can be useful.

Some mentors teach negotiating skills directly or point to resources such as books, workshops, or adept colleagues. But negotiating is also always embedded in the relationship. Mentees can develop their skills in real life in real time this way, and if mentors are empathic, reasonable, and generous, they give their mentees frequent opportunities to practice negotiating. And if a mentor teaches negotiation explicitly, the mentoring relationship can become a safe place to practice conversations for other settings.

 ## The key elements of negotiating

While the most successful negotiators flexibly use a variety of styles, all of us have a preferred style of dealing with conflict. Using the Thomas-Kilmann Conflict Mode Instrument, which was developed to help people understand their preferred conflict styles, Andrea Kupfer Schneider, the professor at Marquette University who is also the resident negotiating expert for the Career Development Institute, has identified five main styles of negotiating.

Based on the Dynamic Negotiating Approach Diagnostic (DYNAD; Schneider & Brown, 2013), styles of negotiation can be classified based on a combination of empathy, assertiveness, and effort or flexibility. Each of the five styles—Competing, Collaborating, Compromising, Avoiding, Accommodating—has its characteristic strategies, power dynamic, and situational advantages and disadvantages. No one style is right for every situation, and none of us feels equally comfortable with all five. Furthermore, each of us has a style we default to in low-intensity situations (the "calm" style) and a style we tend to use in high-intensity situations (the "storm" style). The key is to know yourself and then commit to becoming fluent in the styles that aren't as natural for you. Once you have a few ways to approach negotiations, you'll determine the best style for each negotiation based on the other person's style, the other person's interests, your goals, and the situation overall. We also recommend that mentors and mentees talk about how and when to apply them.

Styles of Negotiating

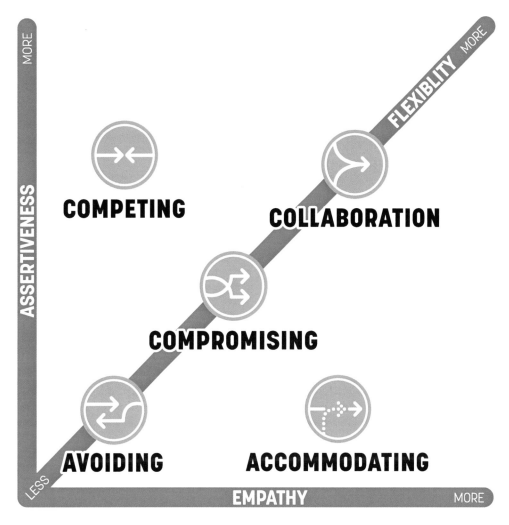

Adapted the book "Smart & Savvy | Negotiation Strategies in Academia" by Andrea Kupfer Schneider and David Kupfer. Used by permission.

Some myths about negotiating

Because we talk so little about negotiating in academia, mentors and mentees might be forgiven for holding some erroneous beliefs about learning and teaching it. Here are a few:

- **Negotiating always means asking a higher-level person to do or give something they don't want to do or give.**
  Negotiating is a part of any relationship, regardless of each person's position or status. Negotiating with a higher-ranking person can be fraught with anxiety for many of us, but luckily, that's only one context. Negotiating often goes smoothly for both parties, involving a simple clarification of needs or desires.

- **Negotiating means arguing.**
  Negotiating can take many tones and include many behaviors. Sometimes it's appropriate to be aggressive, although many times it's not. It's wise to understand the other person's wants, needs, and values and then show them that you have that understanding.

- **Negotiating requires complete calm.**
  Emotions have their place in negotiating. As in many arenas, the goal isn't to avoid or suppress emotion but to regulate it in the service of your goals, and given your partner and situation. One option is to communicate emotions through language (e.g., "I have to admit, I feel frustrated when considering that solution...").

- **Good negotiators feel confident and comfortable when negotiating.**
  There can be discomfort in asking for what you want, experiencing disagreement, or knowing that a request could prompt anger. Expert negotiators are familiar with these experiences, and they're able to tolerate this discomfort.

- **Negotiations always ends with a winner and a loser.**
  This view can make every negotiation feel like a high-stakes undertaking. There are times when a negotiation will end with one party walking away from the table with all the goods, but typically negotiating isn't a zero-sum game.

- **Negotiating requires bravado, a strong case, or a commitment to stick to the original request.**
  These can be appropriate, but there are many approaches. You can enter a negotiation with a range of possible outcomes, you might be focused on a low-stakes (but important) issue, and you could be flexible and curious about your negotiating partner's perspective. You don't have to have 150 percent conviction in the points you'd like to make or a strong sense of injustice to request something.

- **One style of negotiating fits all, regardless of background or identity.**
  We have to be ourselves when negotiating—or dealing with anyone at work—and we must develop negotiating styles and skills accordingly. Gender, age, race/ethnicity, professional level, and physical characteristics all influence the way others perceive us and how we perceive them. Keeping this in mind can help determine the best approach to a particular negotiation.

- **We're born to be good or bad negotiators.**
  Some people certainly feel more comfortable with the back-and-forth of negotiating than others, but training and practice can increase anyone's effectiveness.

- **Negotiating over an issue is a one-time event that ends in a concrete plan.**
  Sometimes a negotiation unfolds over weeks because one or both sides takes time to think, weigh options, and consult others. A willingness to revisit arguments and present new information can turn things around completely.

Promoting the practice of negotiating

Although mentors are likely to have more negotiating experience (as we've noted, this doesn't always translate into more skill), it's possible for both members of the dyad to learn. Addressing the practice of negotiating in direct and concrete terms has benefits for both mentors and mentees.

How can mentors help mentees?

- Teach your mentees how to negotiate. If you have skills, knowledge, and a philosophy about negotiating, talk about them. Point out situations that involve negotiation and discuss specific strategies.

- Use role-playing to help mentees negotiate with others. Help your mentees rehearse, anticipate problems, and approach negotiating partners.

- Give mentees feedback on their negotiations with you. Reflect on what went well (and what didn't) and help your mentee appreciate their strengths and areas where they can improve.

- Share information about your own negotiating strategies, successes, and failures.

- Help mentees learn flexibility in dealing with different people and situations. Mentees might not always recognize how their preferred negotiating style could affect the outcome of a negotiation, and many don't think about how personality and situation come into play.

- On a practical level, if you know someone a mentee will be negotiating with, give mentees information about the other person's style and preferences.

How can mentees learn?

- When choosing a mentor, consider that person's negotiating skills.

- Incorporate negotiating into your training. Make a conscious effort to find formal, mentor-guided, and informal opportunities to learn about negotiating.

- Ask your mentor for tips on what to learn and feedback on how well you've done in recent negotiations. Ask what they wish they'd known at your career stage and what they've learned since.

- Prepare and practice. Clarify your goals and consider what outcomes would satisfy them. Think about your negotiating partner's style, preferences, and reputation. Rehearse with your mentor, peers, or other colleagues.

- Approach negotiations with a relaxed, friendly manner and empathy for the person with whom you'll be negotiating. This can make the other person much more willing to listen.

- Keep a curious attitude. This will show that you're interested in understanding the other person's perspective, not just arguing from your perspective.

How does gender influence negotiating?

Women have traditionally been told that they're too reluctant to ask for resources and that not wanting to negotiate will hurt their long-term chances of succeeding in their careers. Other evidence has suggested that among Millennials, women and men are equally comfortable with negotiating.

Some experts on gender issues in the workplace say that if women want to be competitive in their fields, they have to become comfortable with negotiating—and do it in a new, deliberate way. The assertive behaviors that have traditionally been effective for men, these experts say, can backfire for women, making them vulnerable to labels such as shrill, bossy, or aggressive. Women must negotiate as well as men but differently, entering negotiations aware of the biases inherent in their work culture and the people they negotiate with. Perhaps they have to ask more questions, regulate their emotions more effortfully, use a gentler manner, and smile more frequently than they normally would. This isn't fair, but it can be effective.

Other identity factors—including race, ethnicity, ability, age, socioeconomic status, and LGBTQ+ identity—can also require special strategizing for effective negotiating. Issues of privilege and power are very much at play during a negotiation. Tailoring your preparation to your identity and your negotiating partner's identity is critical.

Like any activity worth doing, negotiation takes practice, determination, focus, and attention. But becoming a better negotiator—and helping others improve their negotiation skills—will serve you well.

Exercise 4 | Are you using negotiating skills optimally?

Dynamic Negotiating Approach Diagnostic (DYNAD)

INSTRUCTIONS: Consider your response in situations where your wishes differ from those of another person. Note that statements A-J deal with your *initial* response to disagreement; statements K-T deal with your response *after the disagreement has gotten stronger*. For consistency, choose one particular conflict setting and use it as background for all the questions. Note that there are no "right" or "wrong" answers; your first impression is usually best. Please refer to the Scoring section (page 133) once you've completed the DYNAD.

Circle one number on the line below each statement for questions A through T.

<- **Not at all Characteristic**   **Very Characteristic** ->

A. WHEN I FIRST DISCOVER THAT DIFFERENCES EXIST,
I make sure that all views are out in the open and treated with equal consideration, even if there seems to be substantial disagreement.

| 1 | 2 | 3 | 4 | 5 | 6 |

B. WHEN I FIRST DISCOVER THAT DIFFERENCES EXIST,
I devote more attention to making sure others understand the logic and benefits of my position than I do to pleasing them.

| 1 | 2 | 3 | 4 | 5 | 6 |

C. WHEN I FIRST DISCOVER THAT DIFFERENCES EXIST,
I make my needs known, but I tone them down a bit and look for solutions somewhere in the middle.

| 1 | 2 | 3 | 4 | 5 | 6 |

D. WHEN I FIRST DISCOVER THAT DIFFERENCES EXIST,
I delay talking about the issue until I have had time to think it over.

| 1 | 2 | 3 | 4 | 5 | 6 |

E. WHEN I FIRST DISCOVER THAT DIFFERENCES EXIST,
I devote more attention to the feelings of others than to expressing my personal concerns.

| 1 | 2 | 3 | 4 | 5 | 6 |

F. WHEN I FIRST DISCOVER THAT DIFFERENCES EXIST,
I am more concerned with goals I believe to be important than with how others feel about the issue.

| 1 | 2 | 3 | 4 | 5 | 6 |

G. WHEN I FIRST DISCOVER THAT DIFFERENCES EXIST,
I often realize that trying to resolve the differences are not worth my effort.

| 1 | 2 | 3 | 4 | 5 | 6 |

H. WHEN I FIRST DISCOVER THAT DIFFERENCES EXIST,
I make sure my goals do not get in the way of our relationship.

| 1 | 2 | 3 | 4 | 5 | 6 |

I. WHEN I FIRST DISCOVER THAT DIFFERENCES EXIST,
I actively explain my ideas and just as actively take steps to understand others' ideas.

| 1 | 2 | 3 | 4 | 5 | 6 |

J. WHEN I FIRST DISCOVER THAT DIFFERENCES EXIST,
I give up some points in exchange for others.

| 1 | 2 | 3 | 4 | 5 | 6 |

K. IF DIFFERENCES PERSIST AND FEELINGS OF CONFLICT ESCALATE,
I set aside my own preferences and become more concerned with keeping the relationship comfortable.

| 1 | 2 | 3 | 4 | 5 | 6 |

L. IF DIFFERENCES PERSIST AND FEELINGS OF CONFLICT ESCALATE,
I refocus discussions and hold out for ways to meet the needs of others as well as my own.

| 1 | 2 | 3 | 4 | 5 | 6 |

M. IF DIFFERENCES PERSIST AND FEELINGS OF CONFLICT ESCALATE,
I let others handle the problem.

| 1 | 2 | 3 | 4 | 5 | 6 |

N. IF DIFFERENCES PERSIST AND FEELINGS OF CONFLICT ESCALATE,
I try to be reasonable by not asking for my full preferences and I make sure I get some of what I want.

| 1 | 2 | 3 | 4 | 5 | 6 |

O. IF DIFFERENCES PERSIST AND FEELINGS OF CONFLICT ESCALATE,
I put forth greater effort to make sure that the truth as I see it is recognized and less on pleasing others.

| 1 | 2 | 3 | 4 | 5 | 6 |

P. IF DIFFERENCES PERSIST AND FEELINGS OF CONFLICT ESCALATE,
I interact less with others and look for ways to find a safe distance.

| 1 | 2 | 3 | 4 | 5 | 6 |

Q. IF DIFFERENCES PERSIST AND FEELINGS OF CONFLICT ESCALATE,
I press for moderation and compromise so we can make a decision and move on.

| 1 | 2 | 3 | 4 | 5 | 6 |

R. IF DIFFERENCES PERSIST AND FEELINGS OF CONFLICT ESCALATE,
I do what needs to be done to resolve the conflict in my favor and hope we can mend feelings later.

| 1 | 2 | 3 | 4 | 5 | 6 |

S. IF DIFFERENCES PERSIST AND FEELINGS OF CONFLICT ESCALATE,
I do what is necessary to soothe the other's feelings.

| 1 | 2 | 3 | 4 | 5 | 6 |

T. IF DIFFERENCES PERSIST AND FEELINGS OF CONFLICT ESCALATE,
I pay close attention to the wishes of others but remain firm that they need to pay equal attention to my wishes.

| 1 | 2 | 3 | 4 | 5 | 6 |

Used with the permission of Andrea Kupfer Schneider.
Schneider, Andrea Kupfer and Gerarda Brown, Jennifer, Dynamic Negotiating Approach Diagnostic (DYNAD) (April 2, 2013). Marquette Law School Legal Studies Paper No. 13-11. Available at https://ssrn.com/abstract=2243679 or http://dx.doi.org/10.2139/ssrn.2243679

CHAPTER 5

Common Challenges in Mentoring

There will be challenges. These challenges will come to young scholars and new mentors, sophisticated fellows and seasoned academics, and everyone in between. They will come when people are new to mentoring, but they can pop up even when both members of the dyad understand exactly what's expected and are deeply committed to working toward success together.

Some are developmental in nature, connected to an individual's career progress or the evolution of the mentor-mentee relationship. The junior professor concerned about getting tenure is likely to experience difficulties—and request help—differently than a seasoned faculty member. And a mentor and mentee who have worked together for three years at the same institution will encounter obstacles unlike those encountered by a pair in which the mentee has just moved 3,000 miles to join the mentor's lab.

Some challenges, such as those caused by mistaken ideas and changing needs, are common, and recognizing them early—or taking preventive action— will help. Others, such as the fallout from serious miscommunication or fundamentally mismatched personalities, require altogether different remedies.

We are not talking here about unprofessional or unethical behavior. That topic is serious and important enough to merit its own discussion in Chapter 8. We can't possibly cover all the challenges dyads face, so here we focus on strategies for dealing with three significant ones. What should mentors and mentees do when one of them has assumptions, presumptions, or views that don't mesh with the other's? What happens when communication breaks down—and how can it be rebuilt? What's the best plan when a pairing is simply a bad match?

Maria, a new faculty member, is frustrated with Laura, an internationally respected scientist who was assigned as her mentor. After moving across the country, Maria hoped Laura would help her get acquainted with the new university's resources, advise her about her first large-scale grant application, and guide her as she starts collecting data. Laura, who travels often, runs a large lab with trainees at every level, and is known more as a visionary than a tactician, meets with Maria as scheduled and gives her some feedback and suggestions, but Maria wants more. She feels neglected: after repeatedly raising the same topics and trying unsuccessfully to schedule more frequent meetings, Maria tells Laura she thinks Laura hasn't fulfilled her mentoring responsibilities.

Laura feels that she has tried to be responsive, answering Maria's many emails between meetings, but by the time Maria complains in person, Laura is losing patience. Maria just seems to need too much. Laura expects her mentees to be independent, and she certainly doesn't intend to rewrite Maria's grant or select her study techniques.

After a candid conversation about expectations, Laura surprises Maria by declaring that the two of them might not be an ideal mentoring match. Maria takes a week to recover but eventually contacts two of Laura's colleagues, as Laura suggested, and she ends up working for the next two years with a more senior, less busy professor who takes time to help Maria broaden her network, develop her ideas, and make decisions about new methods. Perhaps, Maria thinks, Laura wasn't a bad mentor—just not the optimal one for her.

 Case Example 10 | **Helping a Mentee Find the Right Position**

Tina, a mid-career faculty member at a major research university, is frustrated with her mentee Nolan, a postdoctoral fellow in her lab who published several interesting papers during graduate school. Nolan is a talented teacher, but after two years, he's falling short of some traditional research milestones, and Tina and her colleagues are taking note. He takes twice as long as his peers to write a manuscript, and his work, including a grant proposal that he spent six months preparing, is often below par—in the grant's case, receiving a low, unfundable score in peer review. Some colleagues have even said that Nolan's writing and ideas are bland. Tina has discussed these concerns in a candid conversation with Nolan and even asked whether he wants to leave his position. No, Nolan insisted, he plans to stay.

This prompts some soul-searching for Tina. Her other trainees have all had success. Why won't Nolan let her help him by taking her wise advice? Tina eventually realizes that her vision for Nolan is hers—not his—and she makes the difficult switch from wanting Nolan to succeed in her lab to helping him make a graceful exit.

Tina starts by helping Nolan keep the calendar in mind: his fellowship is ending soon, and he needs to think of his next move. A smaller, less research-intensive university might be the best option, Tina says, and she makes sure Nolan knows about job postings and gives him advice as he applies. Tina also discusses Nolan and his strengths with colleagues at other, smaller universities. After a season on the job market, Nolan settles on a tenure-stream position in a mid-tier university that values teaching as well as rigorous research. Thinking ahead to his new workplace, Nolan feels happier in Tina's lab than he's felt in a long time. Years later, both Nolan and Tina look back on Nolan's transition from postdoctoral fellow to respected professor as a smooth one.

Figuring out what their mentees really need was challenging for both Laura and Tina. Questioning their own assumptions and adapting to each mentee's unique path was key, both for their mentees' progress and for their own growth and satisfaction as mentors.

Doing this often involves looking beyond standard measures of success. Maria was making progress, but she was unhappy with the way she and Laura interacted, and she wanted to be directed. Tina had to pause, give up her fantasy of Nolan flourishing in her environment, and think about where his interests and strengths, such as teaching, could take him.

We all look at the world through our own eyes, seeing it through the lens of our personalities and experiences, and it's always more familiar and comfortable to mentor people who are like us in character and career path. But as we have noted, some of the most powerful pairings in mentoring, those that bring great learning and immense satisfaction to both people in the dyad, are those that stretch across differences. These relationships, however, require extra self-awareness on both people's parts and a concerted focus on the mentor's and mentee's goals.

 For Mentors: Strategies for managing challenges

Focus on the mentee's actual—not imagined—career needs

Working with people who have identifiable goals is difficult enough, and this can be extra tough when the goals are unclear, inappropriate, or conflicting with the mentor's wishes. What's more painful is finding that a mentee doesn't know what their goals might be. Sometimes success means helping someone see the facts and make an informed decision. The key is to inquire–and listen–carefully enough to understand what someone really wants and needs.

Give the mentee freedom

Mentees need to explore, finding inspiration in new topics and even considering new career paths. Although it can feel insulting to mentors who hope that mentees will further the mentor's progress, mentors need to give mentees space and a foundation from which to safely explore.

Deal with difficult issues directly

Giving mentees bad news—that their work needs improvement, that they're missing deadlines, or even that they cannot continue in their current position— isn't pleasant. But done in the spirit of caring, such feedback is invaluable.

Address conflict early on—and as part of the relationship

A mentor and a mentee will disagree. Maybe they have different opinions about tasks, deadlines, priorities, and even larger goals. Mentors must maintain professionalism, but they also have the responsibility of figuring out when to compromise, when to agree to disagree, and when to take a stand.

Manage your disappointment

Mentors need to mentor the mentee they have, not the mentee they wish they had. (This is also a challenge in parenting, as Andrew Solomon argues in *Far from the Tree*, his book on children who differ substantially from their parents. One of the most difficult tasks for all parents, Solomon notes, is to accept that their children are not like them.) Mentees will and should take their own paths, and mentors must avoid seeing these choices as a rejection of their values or the effort they've invested.

Help a mentee move on

If a relationship isn't working well, both members of the dyad are responsible for talking about why, difficult as that may be. What changes (if any) would improve the situation? Are the problems practical, such as infrequent or unfocused meetings, or temperamental, stemming from basic approaches to work and success? As with any relationship, if it was worth something at the start, trying to salvage and reconstruct it are good investments. But as in all relationships, it's also important to recognize when problems can't be solved and the best move is a graceful separation. As the more experienced person in the dyad, the mentor should be the one to raise this prospect.

If a mentee is moving on for reasons other than a mismatch, letting go often means loss: loss of the mentee's expertise, enthusiasm, perspective, productivity, collegiality, and even professional and personal bonds. Putting aside one's own feelings and recognizing that the mentee has been there to learn and develop, not to serve the mentor's purposes or further the mentor's work, can require some selflessness and generosity.

For Mentees:
Strategies for managing challenges

Give and receive feedback

Just as mentors need to adapt to those they work with, mentees need to take their cues from their mentors, speaking up (respectfully) when something's not working—and also noting when things are going well. Ultimately, mentees must figure out what works for the relationship, knowledge that will be helpful when they mentor others.

Be clear about expectations and goals

Any mentor might assume that a mentee wants to pursue the path that the mentor followed—or the path that an institution sees as standard. If that's not what the mentee wants, the mentee should do some self-examination and then be candid with the mentor, saying why the traditional or expected path isn't right. Mentees should also speak up about smaller issues, like how and when they'd like feedback on their writing.

Remember that others can help, too

Mentees don't have to restrict themselves to one mentor. Secondary mentors (or a team) can complement the primary mentor's strengths, taking some pressure off the primary relationship. To avoid confusion, it's good for the primary mentor to know what's going on.

For both mentor and mentee:
Set the stage for a fond farewell

Moving to a new location or position or career track, with all the attendant upheaval and uncertainty, can be frightening. It can also be a time when a mentee's emotions about the mentor and the mentoring experience, both pleasant and unpleasant, rise to the surface. Endings are difficult, but try keeping this one in perspective: this is a natural conclusion, the mentee is moving toward greater independence and (everyone hopes) choosing a next step that's consistent with their goals, strengths, and values. If the mentoring experience has been valuable, that's something to celebrate.

But if the relationship isn't working, end it in the most constructive way possible.

If both people involved have done their best to understand why and consider changes, they should have one of those difficult—maybe the most difficult of—conversations. We've seen many mentoring divorces, and the good news is that if the mentor and mentee are candid and clear but also gentle and kind, the ending can be amicable.

We've listed a lot of challenges, and some may feel like enormous setbacks, but we believe that with the right skills, self-awareness, and attention to the other person's experience, you can get through them and be able to sign onto each of the following statements.

Exercise 5 | How well are you managing common challenges?

For Mentors

Check each item that fits your current mentoring experience or approach.

☐ Mentoring is a collaborative effort, and I approach my work with that in mind.

☐ I effectively regulate my emotions so that I can focus on my mentees' training needs rather than my reactions.

☐ When my mentee is frustrated, I try to address their experience directly and compassionately.

☐ I have clear interpersonal limits in my relationships with mentees.

☐ I can put aside my preferences and biases when determining career options for my mentees.

☐ I have found strategies for giving my mentees difficult feedback (e.g., news about poor performance) directly and with empathy.

☐ I can manage difficult conversations with mentees about performance, goals, and plans.

☐ I am committed to my mentees' success, even when it means their goals differ from mine or they are best served by seeking a new position.

☐ When I feel frustrated with a mentee's progress or plans, I am able to evaluate the options for helping them.

☐ I know how to support my mentees in making decisions about changing mentors or career paths.

☐ When conflict arises with a mentee, I have the strategies to manage it.

☐ I am aware of the current challenges I'm experiencing as a mentor and have resources for dealing with them.

For Mentees

Check each item that fits your current mentoring experience or approach.

☐ My mentor and I have clear boundaries for our professional relationship.

☐ When my emotions might interfere with the mentoring relationship, I can identify and regulate them.

☐ When frustration with my mentor arises, I can find a way to address it directly and diplomatically.

☐ I am able to take responsibility when my behavior creates challenges for mentoring.

☐ Achieving my goals means developing more than one mentoring relationship.

☐ When my plans or outcomes don't fit the goals we've developed, I find ways to discuss this with my mentor.

☐ I can prepare for difficult conversations with my mentor by using notes, advice from others, or rehearsal.

☐ Diversity and identity issues influence my experience, my mentor's behavior, and our understanding of each other.

☐ I talk to my mentor about ambivalence or doubts about my career path.

☐ If I decide to change institutions, topics, or career directions, I can get help and support from my mentor.

☐ I have good skills for managing disagreements with my mentor.

☐ When it is time to move on to the next stage of my career, I will be able to work with my mentor to make plans.

CHAPTER 6
Variations on a Theme: Long-Distance, Short-Term, Speed, & Peer Mentoring

Perhaps mentoring has evolved because we now communicate quickly, travel easily, and expect instant results. Whatever the explanation, mentoring exists in different forms to meet our many needs.

Long-distance mentoring, allowing people to connect across time zones, is increasingly common. Short-term mentoring, pairing early-career scientists with more senior colleagues, is popular at professional meetings. Speed mentoring offers an intense, focused experience. Peer mentoring provides guidance and support from someone who shares many of the mentee's current challenges.

These new versions might involve video conferencing, pre-arranged events, timed discussions, or after-work get-togethers, but just like traditional, face-to-face mentoring, they all provide opportunities for growth and reward.

Case Example 11 | Short-Term Mentoring, Long-Term Advantages

Ayana, a graduate student, is nervous about meeting Mark, who has been assigned as her mentor at an international scientific meeting. This is her first time attending the conference, and she's eager to present her own research and learn from others. Ayana and Mark received each other's contact information before the meeting, so Ayana was a little surprised to see that Mark works in government. She wonders whether he'll understand her university research and whether they'll have much in common.

But when they meet, she's pleased to find that Mark is friendly, interested in her goals, and curious about the poster she is to present the next day. Mark is a regular at this scientific meeting, so he knows which scientists in Ayana's field are likely to attend and promises to introduce her to as many of them as possible. Ayana and Mark get together several times during the meeting, including at Ayana's poster presentation, where Mark stops by with colleagues and encourages them to ask about her findings.

On the conference's final day, Mark and Ayana agree to keep in touch, with Mark emphasizing that she's welcome to contact him for more introductions when she applies for postdoctoral positions.

Case Example 12 | **Mentoring Over a Long Distance—with Limits**

Leanne, an associate professor, and Eduardo, a postdoctoral fellow, work at universities separated by three time zones but are participating in a program that provides mentorship for early-stage scientists. Leanne suggests the first few dates for their video chats and in preparation asks Eduardo to send her an outline of a grant proposal he's working on for a deadline that's six months away. She can see that this proposal will require considerable work.

Eduardo always appears on time for their video chats, but he rarely offers much detail about his activities. When he suddenly moves up his timetable for the grant proposal and Leanne presses him for an explanation, she learns that Eduardo's local mentor (a highly regarded scientist who Leanne knows has a reputation for treating mentees like employees) wants him to submit the proposal early so Eduardo can concentrate on one of his mentor's projects. Eduardo says he has to go along with his local mentor's plan. He's lucky to be affiliated with a famous lab, he tells Leanne, and a recommendation from his mentor will be more valuable than any grant of his own.

Leanne tries to explore this challenge with Eduardo: could he discuss the pros and cons of the two deadlines with his local mentor? She suggests some strategies, but Eduardo seems reluctant to use them, so Leanne backs off and ends up focusing on mundane details of Eduardo's work during their chats, praising him for any progress he's made. Leanne doesn't know what she could have done differently, but when the long-distance program ends, she regrets that she didn't give Eduardo more help managing his local mentor.

Ideally, long-distance mentoring can complement local mentoring and even help the mentee address difficulties with a primary mentor, but as Leanne learned, that isn't always the case. Although she gained Eduardo's trust and probably helped him with his day-to-day tasks, Leanne couldn't ease the pressure imposed by his demanding primary mentor.

As Ayana discovered, the benefits of short-term mentoring can be big and long-lasting. She was boosted by Mark's interest, connections, and support, and if Mark, like many senior scientists, enjoys giving others the assistance he once had, he was happy to help someone so young, promising, and enthusiastic.

Traditional mentoring and variations: How do they differ?

FEATURE	TRADITIONAL	LONG-DISTANCE	SHORT-TERM	SPEED	PEER
	TYPE OF MENTORING				
Confidential	☒	☒	☒		☒
Structured	☒	☒	☒	☒	
2-way responsibilities	☒	☒	☒	☒	☒
Focused on mentee's growth	☒	☒	☒		☒
Long duration	☒	☒			
High intensity				☒	
Shared location	☒				☒

What is long-distance mentoring?

Using technologies in various formats, long-distance mentoring can be tailored to meet the needs of those involved. Although the mentor and mentee might be far apart geographically, as Leanne and Eduardo were, they agree to communicate regularly. Logistics vary with the pairings: those involved might hold scheduled meetings, especially at the beginning, or they might converse as needed, perhaps using the time to review the mentee's tasks and challenges. Long-distance mentoring is often arranged as part of a program, as it was for Leanne and Eduardo, but sometimes it springs naturally from the traditional model, such as when a young researcher gets a grant and moves to a new university but keeps her original mentor as the primary mentor on the grant. Some academics who are close to the middle of their careers have multiple, long-term mentors from various phases of their development, all staying in contact across many miles.

Unlike those in a traditional mentoring dyad, a mentor and mentee separated by distance must negotiate the frequency, content, and format of meetings. Most often, the format is video app. Repetition, predictability, and structure are all helpful. The most successful pairings almost always establish a regular meeting time, agree on agendas, and exchange important documents days before they're to be discussed. In contrast to face-to-face meetings, in which body language, familiar surroundings, and the physical setting can lead to a relaxed pace, long-distance discussions require extra efficiency and focus.

Even when long-distance mentoring is working well, the occasional in-person encounter still has value. Email is good for many practical tasks, and talking by phone or video is valuable for more nuanced discussions, but talking in settings like the mentor's lab or a scientific conference are critical for more sophisticated exchanges.

What are long-distance mentoring's benefits and challenges?

Distance can provide objectivity and perspective: when a mentee's work doesn't directly influence the mentor, that mentor's guidance and advice can be especially creative, perhaps encouraging the mentee to ask big questions. Is this a good time to submit a paper or grant? Is this career path really the perfect one? Should I discuss a difficult topic with the local mentor? A long-distance mentor can offer ideas informed by years of experience in other institutions. Discussions about local mentors can be difficult, as Leanne (in this chapter's Case Example) discovered, but the wise long-distance advisor will know how to explore the topic without interfering with that important primary relationship.

Although mentors and mentees working in different locations probably don't have access to the same local grapevines, academia can be a small world, and long-distance mentoring, like the traditional form, should always include agreements about confidentiality that allow the mentee to be frank about goals, challenges, and concerns. The one exception: the long-distance dyad itself, which should not be a secret from another mentor. Long-distance mentoring works best when everyone's in the know.

Probably because our society is so mobile, long-distance mentoring is increasingly becoming many mentees' primary form. But this has drawbacks, especially for a junior-level researcher who's trying to learn critical scholarly or career skills. While it can lead to collaborations involving new topics or new techniques, long-distance mentoring probably isn't the best way for someone to learn and master those novel techniques. And it doesn't always ease the sense of isolation that many young scholars struggle with.

What is short-term mentoring?

By and large, this is mentoring at professional meetings, the kind of conference that Ayana and Mark attended in the Case Example. It's a popular trend: as one colleague recently noted, "it seems every time I sneeze, a professional society asks me to be a mentor at their annual meeting." Others call these mentoring experiences "weekend wonders."

Short-term mentoring has become common for good reason: it offers newcomers a chance to meet an expert (and usually established) colleague, get guidance, and meet other leaders and potential collaborators (or mentors) all in one place and within a short time.

By definition, this mentoring is brief and more casual than traditional same-location mentoring, more like a blind date with low expectations. The mentor and mentee are often paired by a third party, perhaps based on their topic areas or the mentee's expressed needs. The mentor and mentee interact over a few days, often as part of a structured program. They're sometimes expected to attend formal events, such as a mentor-mentee luncheon with a panel or speaker, and to meet individually as needed.

What are short-term mentoring's benefits and challenges?

Short-term mentoring can be limited to a brief encounter or—as seemed likely for Ayana and Mark in the Case Example—can turn into a longer-term association. As with long-distance mentoring, a short-term mentor sometimes has a valuable, disinterested perspective, which can let the mentor zero in on the mentee's needs and goals. Because of its time frame, this short-term arrangement usually focuses on quick, concise advice.

Short-term mentoring has benefits for both involved: in the best-case scenarios, mentees are introduced to experienced scholars, and mentors can meet rising stars, contribute to a junior colleague's career development, and generally give back to their fields. Although most short-term mentoring ends with the conference's last day, some short-term mentors and mentees choose to keep in touch and even collaborate.

On the pitfall side, short-term mentoring might not be mentoring at all. Quality control can be a problem: since mentors usually just sign up for (or are assigned to) a conference's mentoring program, they might not have the training or commitment to really help mentees, or they might be more interested in getting attention from the professional society than providing substantial assistance. Because conferences are big events with many attendees and many social opportunities, confidentiality can be a concern, especially when current colleagues are present and future recommendations can be at stake.

Matching can cause problems, too. If this hasn't been done well, the mentor and mentee might already know each other, lack common interests, or not get along. Interactions between the mentor and mentee also might not be sufficiently structured. Not every association or organization provides guidelines for what's expected.

All these concerns make us wonder: is short-term mentoring true mentoring? Often it resides somewhere at the intersection of advice, networking, and mentoring. Committed, mentee-focused mentoring might be rare, but maybe that's not always the point. Instead, the goals could be to meet a new colleague, have a conference tour guide, and expand a professional network.

The American College of Neuropsychopharmacology (ACNP), an organization both of us are involved in, sets a good example of how to do short-term mentoring, providing mentors with guidelines, recommended tasks, and ways to have meaningful interactions. The ACNP considers mentoring important enough to track and consider when weighing the promotion of members to fellow status.

Excerpts of the ACNP's step-by-step suggestions for mentees

1 | Before the annual meeting

Mentees are encouraged to identify three to five senior scientists who are ACNP members or will be attending the meeting to facilitate the ACNP mentor in helping the mentee meet and network with leaders in their field.

2 | During the annual meeting

Mentees are encouraged to meet with their ACNP mentor on multiple occasions, including during their poster or oral presentation.

3 | After the annual meeting

Mentees should contact their ACNP mentor to schedule quarterly phone conferences and prepare an agenda for those discussions. Mentees are encouraged to consult with their ACNP and primary mentors about symposium presentations for future ACNP meetings and with their ACNP mentor about expectations for associate and full membership in the ACNP.

General suggestions for mentors

- Ask about your mentee's current position, short-term goals, and long-term plans.

- Assess your mentee's progress and provide guidance on how to continue it.

- Introduce your mentee to colleagues who could be collaborators or mentors.

General suggestions for mentees:

- Approach this as a chance to meet a valued colleague, get some quick career advice, and possibly form a relationship outside your local mentoring.

- Use your mentoring time well: show up on time, have some questions prepared, and get right to the point about the advice you'd like to receive.

- After the conference, be sure to thank the mentor for their time and effort.

What is speed mentoring?

Speed mentoring, which involves a series of five- to 10-minute conversations between mentors and mentees and often occurs at conferences or training events, is akin to speed dating. An organizer opens the proceedings, provides ground rules, and runs a timer to make sure that people move when their scheduled conversation ends.

Participants often sit on either side of a long table, and those on one side of the table (often mentors) stay put while those on the other side (often mentees) move one seat down every time the conversation alarm sounds. In other instances, each mentor stays in an assigned location and mentees come and go. However things are structured, the goal is for mentors and mentees to meet in as many pairings as possible in a short time.

What's on your T-shirt?

...is a question David often poses to trainees. In other words, can you telegraph who you are and what you do?

The answer should last less than 15 seconds and be so pithy it could fit legibly on a T-shirt. Speed mentoring is a great setting for your T-shirt speech, so have one.

What are speed mentoring's benefits and challenges?

Speed mentoring is innovative and engaging, but it definitely has disadvantages. The process is structured, but its content can vary, and it can end up being merely an introduction or a name game ("Do you know...?"). The setting can be too crowded to allow mentees to describe their goals and difficulties comfortably. The mood of the room is often rushed, a bit giddy, or even scattered, so those participating might end up laughing (genuinely or nervously) more than talking.

Time pressure, which is the very nature of speed mentoring, can make both mentors and mentees feel an urgency about getting to important material. The pairings might not be carefully organized, so mentees might meet mentors whom they already know or share few interests with.

Our suggestion is to approach speed mentoring as a fun social event rather than a chance for deep, personalized guidance. If you talk with someone whose expertise, perspective, and interpersonal style fit yours, that's a bonus. If you're lucky enough for the stars to align so that the environment, pairings, and conversations suit you, you might even get a little wisdom. In that case, you can share contact information and maybe get some real mentoring later.

Suggestions for mentors

- Arrive armed with focused advice. Consider what you think mentees need to know, how you've succeeded, and where the field is going.

- Encourage the mentee to guide the interaction and ask questions, rather than making things didactic.

- Be mindful of the interaction's brief nature, guiding the discussion to a close as the time limit approaches.

Suggestions for mentees

- Be prepared. Rehearse a 30-second introduction with your name, institution, training background, position, and topic area (see the T-Shirt box on the previous page).

- Make a list of questions, focusing on general advice or specific tasks. For example, "When I start job hunting, what are the most important criteria for evaluating departments?"

- Bring note-taking materials so you can write down any wise suggestions.

- Set your expectations toward adventure rather than depth.

What is peer mentoring?

This is just what its name suggests. Unlike the typical mentor, who's most often at a more advanced career stage than the mentee, peer mentors are approximately at the mentee's own level. This gives them a firsthand perspective on what's expected and an empathy for everyday struggles, obstacles, and triumphs. Optimism, enthusiasm for attaining goals, and excitement about others' accomplishments are big plusses. Healthy, team-mate competitiveness can be helpful, but anxious, zero-sum-game competitiveness isn't.

Peer mentoring can occur informally, as it might for two junior faculty members who're both working toward a career development grant submission with the same deadline and hold weekly goal-setting sessions. It can evolve into a group activity, as is the case for Erika's Neurochicks group at the University of Pittsburgh, which began as a weekly happy hour for mid-to-senior-level female neuroscientists and now involves sharing support for career challenges, comparing notes on research activities, and even devising collaborations. It can even be a formal activity from the outset, one in which a group of carefully selected members from one workplace meets regularly, with a detailed agenda and designated rotating leader.

What are peer mentoring's benefits and challenges?

When two individuals are on similar schedules, have the same background, and share career goals, they can feel insecure over the possibility that only one will succeed. If they're entering the job market at the same time or applying for limited resources, they might feel awkward about sharing information, or admitting their self-doubts. But that isn't always the reality: a close colleague who's facing similar challenges in a similar climate can provide tremendous instrumental and emotional support. One person's success doesn't mean the other's failure. Instead, colleagues can inspire, encourage, and help, exchanging drafts of work, offering suggestions for improvement, providing information about opportunities, and boosting low spirits. Sometimes the best mentors are people at the same level.

A challenge: for a junior-level academic, peer mentors might lack the networks, reputation, and resources of senior-level mentors. They haven't been in the field or industry long enough to know its ups and downs or why some succeed.

Suggestions for mentors and mentees

- Hold regular meetings, even if infrequent. Treat this like any mentoring arrangement.

- Allow for some flexibility in content and roles, letting people switch between the roles of mentor and mentee as needed and addressing topics as they arise.

- Try to keep mentoring somewhat separate from friendship. Friendship is a wonderful foundation for the trust and openness of effective mentoring, but plan to have drinks, take a walk, or see a movie another time.

Mentoring in its many forms helps everyone—whether they're separated by distance, meeting at an event, or working at the same institution. Here are some questions to ask as mentoring gets underway, ones tailored to the context of each type of mentoring.

Exercise 6 | How should you approach non-traditional mentoring?

LONG-DISTANCE MENTORING

FOR MENTOR	FOR MENTEE	FOR BOTH
■ What are your broad career goals?	■ What are your thoughts on my research topic?	■ What's the best way for us to communicate?
■ What is and isn't going well now?	■ Do my goals seem feasible?	■ How will this mentoring experience fit into the mentee's current, primary mentoring?
■ What are your current research interests and plans?	■ How can I work more effectively with my current, primary mentor?	

SHORT-TERM MENTORING

FOR MENTOR	FOR MENTEE	FOR BOTH
■ What are your research topic and career goals?	■ How can I be most effective at reaching my current goals?	■ What depth of guidance is feasible in this context?
■ Which deadlines or goals are looming in the next year?	■ Are there topics, techniques, or methods you'd suggest I incorporate?	■ Does it make sense to stay in contact?
■ Is there anyone you'd especially like to meet at this conference or event?	■ Are there career resources you'd recommend?	

SPEED MENTORING

FOR MENTOR	FOR MENTEE	FOR BOTH
■ What is the focus of your research?	■ What's your advice on succeeding at this stage of my academic career?	■ What challenges or interests do we have in common?
■ What is your current career stage?	■ Do you have suggestions about my research topic or technique?	■ What general wisdom will be useful?
■ What are your most pressing questions about your career progress?	■ What steps should I take to prepare for my next career transition?	

PEER MENTORING*

FOR MENTOR	FOR MENTEE	FOR BOTH
■ What kind of feedback would help you make progress?	■ Am I missing anything important in my current work?	■ Will we focus on the content of our current projects or the process of completing them?
■ Which steps have you taken to reach your current goals?	■ What's the best way to set short-term and long-term goals?	■ How can we keep personal conversation from taking over?
■ How are you approaching the major challenges of our career stage?	■ What are the best resources for career development advice?	

*In peer mentoring, both members of the dyad can play the role of mentor or mentee, so the suggested questions could be used by either member.

CHAPTER 7
Diversity & Mentoring

Does your mentor have to look like you or share your racial, ethnic, religious, family, or socioeconomic background? As a mentor, can you work effectively with a mentee who has a perspective or identity vastly different from yours? How can mentoring foster diversity and inclusion, and also promote equity and justice in academia?

For decades, mentors have been white men who trained white men. As academia is working to become more diverse—and to value the higher-quality scholarship that comes with diversity—mentors remain largely white and male, while mentees have increasingly come from other groups. Today, as David notes, even though mentors can come from various backgrounds, the people at the top of our field, academic psychiatry, remain, as a group, "too male, pale, and frail." We need to ensure diversity throughout the levels of academic institutions to reap its very real benefits.

Many groups are less than ideally represented in academia, although this depends on the field. Some areas such as physics, for example, suffer more gender imbalance than others, such as psychology. When we refer to under-represented groups, we're thinking of groups that are disproportionately not included in our academic workforce and encounter bias and discrimination that prevents their inclusion and damages the workforce. Women, BIPOC (Black, Indigenous, and People of Color), people with physical or mental disabilities, those who grew up in very low-resource environments, and people who identify as LGBTQ+ are among the groups considered under-represented, but members of other groups can also have less-than-ideal representation.

When the male, pale, and frail choose the mentees they feel most comfortable mentoring, they often select those who are similar (although perhaps not always as frail). They might not be aware of this bias, or they might justify their choice based on other qualifications, interests, or characteristics. But this approach perpetuates privilege for their group.

Mentoring people who have different perspectives and backgrounds isn't just fair. It improves our academic work, since collaborators with a wide range of backgrounds tend to produce more creative, effective solutions than those who are all alike. It also makes our communities smarter and more talented: by mentoring diverse individuals, we help ensure that each academic field will be populated by people of the highest ability from every group, not just people of varying ability from only one group.

Finding ways to promote and encourage junior academics from under-represented groups can be difficult. In this chapter, we tackle the emerging approaches to this critical issue of contemporary mentoring.

 ## Case Example 13 | **Getting Past the Discomfort of Differences**

Ruth, an early-career academic, is generally pleased with the mentoring she has received. Jay, a full professor in her department, has given Ruth opportunities to work on high-profile projects, and he always makes sure she gets credit. Jay and Ruth have many career, scholarly, and personal interests in common, and if asked, each would say that they feel respected by the other. They have not, however, discussed one big topic: the differences in their experiences and backgrounds.

Ruth is Black, identifies as female, and is in her early 30s. Jay, a white man, is in his late 50s. They experience their workplace very differently: Ruth, the only person of color in their large research group, sometimes feels lonely and misunderstood, and she has been offended by some colleagues' comments about race and achievement. Jay, who has worked at the university for decades, is not oblivious to Ruth's difficulties, but he isn't sure how or even whether he can help.

In one of their regular meetings, Ruth finally raises the topic of race and identity. She emphasizes that she's not criticizing Jay but tells him that feeling different from others is a part of her daily experience that often makes completing her work more difficult. Jay is uncomfortable at first but acknowledges that he hasn't done much to help Ruth in this area—and that he would like to do more. At first, Jay is tempted to ask Ruth to help him understand, but he realizes that such an approach would put even more pressure on her. He acknowledges that the responsibility to understand and act belongs with him. Because he still feels as if he knows little about the ways he might have contributed to the interpersonal or institutional burden on a talented young scholar in an already demanding position, Jay decides to take a deliberate, scholarly approach. He reads about antiracism, joins a faculty group focused on addressing racism, and asks others in his university how he can understand the experience of BIPOC colleagues. During his mentoring interactions with Ruth, he now sometimes stops to ask if an action or comment came across as hurtful or dismissive. Ruth, glad that she has taken initiative, looks forward to Jay's efforts to bring up topics of difference and promote a more inclusive atmosphere.

 ## Case Example 14 | **Discovering Bias**

Ian is a trainee in Christina's lab at a large university, a big group that includes four other postdoctoral fellows as well as residents, graduate students, and undergraduates. Christina has built a diverse team and is known as a supportive mentor for trainees from under-represented backgrounds. At one of his first meetings with the group, Ian, who is the only white, male, straight, cisgender trainee in the lab, complains about the difficulties faced by white men. Another trainee, who is female and Latinx, responds that whatever white men must grapple with today is very different from the problems of people who have never been part of the main, privileged group. Ian laughs and seems not to notice that the female trainee feels insulted.

Ian startles Christina with other statements: in one of their regular meetings, he notes with disdain that the director of the National Institutes of Health recently announced he will turn down invitations to any scientific meeting where he'd be serving on a "manel." Ian points out that a recent scientific meeting he and Christina attended included several all-women panels. He asks, Aren't all-female panels just as offensive?

Christina isn't sure whether Ian's comments reveal sexism, a genuine concern about fairness, or just a wish to be provocative. After some consideration, she opts for a direct approach and in a private meeting asks Ian whether he's concerned about men losing status as women gain visibility and equity. When he answers with a shrug, Christina urges him to consider how his experiences and identity could be interfering with his understanding of how bias can affect scientists' careers, and she suggests some resources on the topic. Ian sees himself as an ally of under-represented scientists, but not wanting to alienate his mentor, he does some reading and takes an online implicit bias test that delivers some stark news: he has a strong bias against women in general and women of color in particular. Slowly but thoughtfully, he starts giving more consideration to his opinions and actions at work.

As these examples illustrate, different identities and varying points of view can create misunderstanding, confusion, and at times discomfort for mentors and mentees—but these differences can also allow for opportunities to learn together and from one another.

 ## How do gender, race, ethnicity, sexual orientation, transgender identity, and socioeconomic status influence academic career development?

As we have noted, it's no secret that power and leadership in academia have long been held by white heterosexual men and that women, BIPOC, anyone with an LGBTQ+ identity, and people with disabilities haven't had equal opportunities to succeed. Another group that often goes unrecognized is people from low socioeconomic backgrounds, especially when their families have lived in poverty for generations and have had little upward financial mobility. Role models are crucial for people building careers, and those from poorly represented groups who are moving up the academic status ladder see few at the top who share their identity.

Challenges to career success and growth are many and varied. They include overt discrimination such as racism, implicit bias (which is unconscious), clueless homophily (preference for those who are like ourselves, which leads, for example, to white men helping other white men), and internalized stigma (e.g., a person with sexual minority identity experiencing homophobia turned inwardly). Being from any group that has been traditionally underrepresented may mean that you're a trailblazer, but perhaps also lonely or uninitiated in the academic world. It can also mean that others are openly hostile toward you, don't know how to behave around you, or simply don't understand you.

One unfortunate result is that people from under-represented backgrounds can feel pressure to appear perfect, to represent their entire group, and to prove that they're deserving. As many BIPOC colleagues have said, "you have to be twice as good to be seen as half as competent." Mentees from under-represented or non-traditional backgrounds might feel as though they have fewer chances to fall and get back up—which might often be the case and can contribute to high attrition rates in academia. When these challenges make young people reluctant to admit insecurity or ask for support, the pressure can increase and the chances of succeeding can decline. People from under-represented groups can become self-protective, discouraged, and isolated, all of which can be serious liabilities in academia.

 ## How can mentors help?

Mentors from more traditional backgrounds can do at least three things to provide for their mentees from under-represented groups. They can share their privilege, both the kind that is earned and the sort that is automatically conferred by their identity, by offering funding, resources, and access to their professional networks. They can also be advocates, promoting their mentees by nominating them for awards, including them in high-profile projects, praising them to colleagues, and giving their work public credit in presentations. Finally, mentors can develop their own awareness of racism, bias, and privilege through education and process groups, which can provide the necessary skills for addressing these issues directly with and for their mentees (see the Resources section).

Mentors can learn—and make it a priority—to become comfortable and active about asking their mentees about their experiences of bias and discrimination, as Jay finally did with Ruth in this chapter's Case Example. This helps mentors understand the experiences of mentees from other groups, take steps to identify and address inequities, and if needed, step in to change mentees' experiences.

If a young scholar is from an under-represented group, should a mentor be from that same group?

A mentor who shares the mentee's background and identity, someone who might have experienced bias or discrimination, can provide validation as well as practical advice on how to navigate systems in an institution or field. Having a mentor who shares your identity can remove some pressure to maintain an image of perfection, composure, or total self-sufficiency. All the same, it is unreasonable based on the composition of the academic workforce to expect that all mentees from under-represented groups could find mentors from their groups. This reinforces the need for mentors from male, pale, and frail (or well-represented) groups to prepare to mentor people who are indeed different from them. Mentors can also help by offering resources, access to established colleagues, and the kind of power that can address inequities.

Women's mentors, we believe, needn't all be women. Men can leverage their powerful positions to be allies and advocates for female mentees. Women need and deserve committed mentors.

As we have recommended several times for other reasons, assembling a team of mentors, including mentors from under-represented as well as traditionally high-status groups, offers opportunities for resources as well as learning. Our answer to this one (like so many others)? Diversify your mentoring team.

 Does a mentor have to deal with a mentee's identity explicitly?

Our stance is that this should be done both explicitly and implicitly. An effective mentor will be open to hearing concerns about inclusion, examples of biased behavior (by the mentor and by others), and suggestions for ensuring fair treatment. In some cases, the most important factor is action to promote and maintain equitable treatment.

Most people who have been in academia for decades have settled in and probably feel that they've earned all their success. But those who want to be good mentors should take note that not everyone has this experience. Many of us suffer from imposter syndrome, the nagging belief that we don't deserve to be where we are. This can take an acute form for people from groups not traditionally represented in the academy, and it's important for these individuals and their mentors to acknowledge the thoughts and emotions that accompany this syndrome. It's also important to remind yourself—whether you're the mentor or mentee—that you deserve to be where you are, regardless of any lingering self-doubt.

Career challenges are common to women across fields of science, as noted in a compelling 2013 New York Times Magazine article by Eileen Pollack headlined "Why Are There Still So Few Women in Science?" The author, who was one of the first women to receive an undergraduate degree in physics from Yale, expressed surprise at today's strong, seemingly unchanged bias against women in science. As she sees it, the poor representation of women results from a combination of academics viewing science as a male profession, women's seemingly (or more easily acknowledged) low confidence, and the clear inequities in resources, including pay and lab space. Encouragement could be more influential for women than men, so one big step toward gender equity could be providing stronger mentoring for women.

How does geographic origin come into play?

How does geography affect our experience and perceptions? Does someone who grew up in a rural setting see the world differently than a city dweller or suburbanite? What about religious upbringing? Will an atheist behave differently from someone raised in a deeply religious environment? Can someone from a coastal region really understand a Midwesterner? Such differences are little studied but important, and we urge both mentors and mentees to consider these forms of identity when working to develop a culture of inclusion and equity.

Suggestions for mentors

■ **Encourage diversity in your academic group.**
Pay attention to the identities and areas of expertise represented across your team. In lab meetings and conference presentations, make sure to center the voice by giving opportunities to those not adequately represented in science.

■ **Use equitable practices when selecting mentees for tasks, projects, or perks.**
Don't always ask for volunteers, assume who'll be best for the task, or reward the most vocal person. Notice who's working on what and whether the distribution is fair.

■ **Don't wait for mentees from under-represented groups to find you.**
Make an effort to identify and recruit mentees from under-represented backgrounds. Ask mentees to nominate peers, contact interest groups in your professional organizations, and approach early-career academics who've given impressive papers or posters at conferences.

- **Educate yourself about the challenges that less-privileged mentees or groups face.**
  It's not your mentee's job to help you understand bias and privilege and work to promote equity. This responsibility falls to you, the person in the mentoring relationship with more power and privilege.

- **Protect your mentees from distractions.**
  Having members who are women, BIPOC, and others who have less status can make a committee look good, but committee work can take effort and attention away from career-promoting activities. A mentor can help a mentee by encouraging the mentee to choose carefully and say no often, to avoid helping a university or institution achieve its diversity goals at the expense of the mentee's career.

 ## Suggestions for mentees

- **Find and join a lab or research group that is not homogeneous.**
  This suggests that the mentor appreciates or even works to build an inclusive group.

- **Choose your battles.**
  As the primary goals for a mentee are to finish training, become an independent scholar, or excel in your field, focus on the supports and strategy needed to achieve this goal. Pointing out challenges to equity and inclusion is important and can happen in many ways. As BIPOC scientists have noted, it can be counterproductive to your goals to always be the person highlighting discrimination. To obtain support, consider communicating concerns to a diversity committee, another mentor, or a senior investigator you trust.

- **Speak up for those who face unfair treatment.**
  If you're not from an under-represented group, you can still be an ally. If you witness bias or discrimination in action, your privilege can give you a voice and an opportunity that others may not have. If you care about equity, you can help promote it.

Dealing with diversity, as a mentor or mentee, is an everyday challenge, one that many people are uncomfortable discussing. But this is work worth doing—to improve our environment, our work, and our world.

Exercise 7 | How well are you addressing diversity, equity, and inclusion?

FOR BOTH MENTORS & MENTEES

Describe your background and identity in one or two sentences.

What are the advantages and challenges of your background?

■ Advantages:

■ Challenges:

What are some things you don't understand about the role of diversity in mentoring?

Have you taken an implicit bias test (see Resources for a link)?
What have you learned about your own biases?

How do you respond when you experience or witness biased treatment of others?

How could you improve your strategy for addressing diversity and inclusion in mentor-mentee relationships?

For Mentors

Check each item that fits your current mentoring experience or approach.

☐ I have implemented methods to enhance the diversity of my research team.

☐ I am able to talk with my mentees about their identities and backgrounds and how those have influenced their professional experiences.

☐ It is necessary to tolerate discomfort when discussing difficult but important issues involving diversity, inclusion, and equity.

☐ We all have unconscious biases and blind spots. I try to identify mine.

☐ I can address bias and discrimination directly with my mentees.

☐ At the departmental or institutional level, I am aware of the ways that bias and discrimination influence mentees.

☐ The privilege I experience can make it challenging for me to understand the bias or discrimination that others experience.

☐ In order to cultivate open discussion, I am willing to acknowledge my mistakes or inadvertently upsetting statements as part of talking about diversity issues.

☐ Listening and curiosity, rather than a wish to be correct or have expertise, are critical for understanding the experiences of others.

☐ I consider myself an ally of my mentees who are from under-represented groups or experience bias because of their identity.

☐ I try to anticipate and provide the type of encouragement and support that mentees from different backgrounds need to succeed in my field.

☐ Even if mentees don't directly raise issues about diversity, inclusion, and equity, I try to be aware of them and make it clear that I'm willing to discuss them.

For Mentees

Check each item that fits your current mentoring experience or approach.

☐ My background or identity has influenced my career goals and my expectations about success.

☐ I am aware of how my own biases influence my behavior at work.

☐ My background and identity influence my role and functioning in my mentor's team.

☐ My mentor endeavors to understand my perspective and experiences as they influence my training and career development.

☐ I can talk with my mentor about equity in our organization, my experiences of bias or discrimination, and our different perspectives.

☐ My mentor tries to understand my unique challenges in the context of our research group, institution, and field.

☐ I can ask for my mentor's support and guidance when addressing an experience of bias or discrimination.

☐ I have sought out mentors who can appreciate the challenges I've experienced because of similar experience or commitment to learning about equity.

☐ For mentees from under-represented groups, there can be benefits to having mentors from both under-represented backgrounds and traditional backgrounds.

☐ I have developed skills in raising concerns about inclusion and equity while maintaining a strong relationship with my mentor.

CHAPTER 8
Professional Behavior

Ethical breaches in the workplace are nothing new, but the awareness of inappropriate and even criminal behavior, especially as experienced by women, has grown dramatically in recent years. The #MeToo era's increased openness and urgency have made us all aware of the serious costs to those on the receiving end of such behavior: personal suffering, loss of security and comfort in work, and careers curtailed or even destroyed.

A case at the University of Rochester is a particularly alarming example of inappropriate behavior in academia—and an institution's insufficient response. A complaint to the Equal Employment Opportunity Commission filed by faculty and graduate students in 2017 described a faculty member as a "narcissistic and manipulative sexual predator" and detailed his sexual relationships, harassing comments, and distribution of graphic photos. Other Rochester faculty members said that the university investigated the case lamely, exonerating the faculty member and promoting him to full professor while the investigation was in progress. In response, more than 1,000 people in the cognitive neuroscience field took the extraordinary step of publicly vowing to discourage their students from seeking training at the University of Rochester. The University of Rochester has never found this faculty member guilty of harassment, and it wasn't until March 2020 that it agreed to a $9.4 million settlement in a lawsuit claiming that it had retaliated against the women making the claims. Progress has been slow and, in many ways, frustrating.

Inappropriate behavior occurs at every level, but when it happens to early-stage academics who might fear retaliation or damage to their growing reputations, addressing it can be especially difficult. The real issue is power. Outside of work, turning down someone's advance might lead to hurt feelings or frosty future meetings. Doing so inside a university or institution, where older, established academics have great influence, can be downright dangerous.

Case Example 15 | **Unwanted Attention**

Aoife, an associate professor at a research university, is finding that attending conferences often includes awkward and even threatening experiences. Once, an older male colleague propositioned her as they waited for an elevator. On another occasion, a colleague commented that he'd like to join Aoife for dinner because she was wearing a short skirt. (When she expressed surprise, he said, with a shocked expression, "I was kidding!") In recent years, she has spent her time avoiding a third colleague who seems to mysteriously turn up next to her at conference sessions, bump into her at receptions, and walk into the hotel fitness center just as she starts her workout. She has tried to make her wishes known by walking away, saying she isn't interested, and once or twice asking, "Did you really just do that?" Aoife is proud of herself—being assertive has been difficult—although she isn't sure her actions have been very effective. She also knows that so far she's fared better than two close colleagues who left academia because their mentors made sexual remarks or demanded sexual favors. But at times she still doesn't feel safe traveling alone, and her fears are limiting her efforts to take on high-profile roles in professional associations.

When Aoife tells her mentor Steve about the colleague who makes her uncomfortable at conferences, Steve sees it as unwanted romantic attention, telling her to just brush it off. Aoife is disappointed by Steve's response: in addition to being unsympathetic, he ignores the factors of power imbalance and intimidation, since the colleague in question has been a faculty member in their university for decades. But because they have an otherwise excellent relationship, Aoife doesn't pursue the topic with Steve.

Instead she seeks advice from colleagues who have been informal mentors and advisors, including women who she knows have also experienced unwanted attention. Some are men who have dealt with sexual harassment in their administrative roles. These conversations are very helpful: Aoife gets guidance and feels validated. These colleagues assure Aoife that her experiences are not just minor hassles, that she isn't overreacting, and that the encounters are worth addressing. The senior colleague's behavior, Aoife decides, has reached the threshold of meriting a formal complaint, and she begins to gather information for reporting it. She is grateful that others appreciate her struggle.

Case Example 16 |
Addressing Troubling Behavior

Helena, an associate professor at a large university, is surprised when Dawn, an assistant professor and Helena's mentee, arrives at their regular meeting visibly shaken. Dawn tells Helena that when she was trying to start a session for her research project earlier that day, John, one of her colleagues, exploded in anger, screaming at her in front of one of the participants in her study. It started with a mixup over group resources: Dawn had reserved a shared research room, so she was surprised when John suddenly appeared, shouted that he needed the room immediately, and demanded that she get out. When Dawn tried to discuss this misunderstanding with John later, he again lost his temper and accused her of interfering with his work.

Helena is well aware of John's temper and tendency to treat his mentees and junior colleagues with contempt—although to Helena's surprise, many of her colleagues consider his actions merely quirky. She has vowed to help protect her mentees from his bullying, but this has been challenging. The last time she told senior colleagues about threats John made during an outburst, they said only, "Oh, he's harmless. He never follows through."

Helena reassures Dawn that John's behavior was out of line. How does Dawn want to proceed? Helena says that since John hasn't owned up to his misconduct in the past, she would like to address this with him briefly, but then plan to take it up the chain of command. When John responds as expected, Helena and Dawn decide to discuss John's original outburst and later response, along with some similar events, with their department's vice chair. The department launches an investigation that ends with formally notifying John that his behavior with Dawn was unacceptable and he must keep away from her as much as their work allows. If he retaliates against Dawn or anyone else, the department chair tells John, he'll face serious disciplinary consequences. From then on, John avoids Dawn.

As Dawn learned, unprofessional behavior often occurs in private, with no witnesses or potential defenders. She benefitted from Helena's support, but not all young scholars have mentors who believe them and are willing to take on a colleague. Many who behave inappropriately, like John, have long histories of bad behavior, targeting lower-status colleagues and bullying people into silence while somehow managing to convince their bosses that they're harmless, so getting people in power to take action against these individuals, especially after years of looking the other way, can feel like a losing battle.

Mentees who experience inappropriate behavior should speak up, and mentors who witness or hear about it should defend their mentees, asking for clarification and explanation as needed (as Steve, the Case Example mentor, did not). Neither is easy, but we have suggestions for identifying and responding to inappropriate behavior.

 ## What is appropriate behavior?

On their own interpersonal level, mentors and mentees should always treat each other (and everyone else in their work environment) with respect and courtesy. At a minimum, this includes polite language, a focus on work during conversations, and decency during all interactions. There should also be fairness without favoritism. Mentors should treat staff, mentees, and colleagues with a common level of respect. Local cultural norms can influence the definition of acceptable and inappropriate, and both members of the mentoring dyad are responsible for knowing and observing what's allowed—and what's not.

 ## What's inappropriate behavior?

Whatever the norms and local customs, when something's not right, people—especially those who are on the receiving end—know it.

Some behaviors are so extreme that everyone agrees they're wrong. Cruel criticism, personal attacks, belittling treatment, sexual comments, physical contact, statements about personal or physical characteristics, and making professional advancement contingent on a personal relationship have no place in the mentoring relationship or anywhere elsewhere in academia. Predatory behavior—such as aggressive, repeated, and persistent romantic or sexual advances that stem from greed, low empathy, and a high need for control by someone with more power—is a particularly pernicious problem.

Mentors should be aware of these unacceptable behaviors (for themselves as well as others) but should be on the lookout for other, less obvious mistreatment and believe someone who details bad behavior that happened in private. What seems like acceptable (or perhaps just familiar?) behavior to one person, like Steve's interpretation of the creepy colleague's approaches to Aoife at conferences, might be completely offensive to another. Asking good questions with an open mind will help.

There are other levels of bad behavior: neglecting or ignoring someone can be impolite at best and undermining at worst. This can include failing to return emails, read written products, contribute to projects, and observe deadlines.

 ## How does implicit bias fit in?

Research on implicit bias—the tendency to respond differently to others based on their identity or characteristics that occurs outside of one's own awareness—has burgeoned in recent years and has raised difficult questions. How do we assess such bias? Once we discover it, what, if anything, can we do to improve our actions?

The answer, we think, lies in embracing diversity and aiming for self-awareness that translates into fair behavior. If mentors consciously seek out and work with people who are very different from themselves, in background, identity, and experience, they will learn much about their own implicit biases as well as how others see and walk through the world.

Varieties of mentors' inappropriate behavior

The following are some, but not all, of the types of inappropriate behavior that can occur in mentoring (as well as academia in general).

■ **Discrimination**

This has fairly clear legal and ethical definitions and implications. Favoring mentees based on race, gender, religion, age, or LGBTQ+ identity when hiring, assigning projects, providing resources, nominating colleagues for awards, or sharing your professional network is clearly wrong. At the same time, discrimination can be difficult to prove. Examples include departments that pay male faculty more than female faculty at the same level, with the excuse that individual qualifications and achievements vary, precluding comparisons by gender.

■ **Romantic or sexual behavior**

The danger of any romantic or sexual relationship between mentor and mentee is that what can seem consensual (especially to the party with greater power in the relationship) might not be—as in the case with sexual harassment—or could be tainted by lopsided power. To those who ask "can't people fall in love at work?" we answer, "it's acceptable, as long as the two people have equal rank and power or change their circumstances so that's the case." Our blanket advice: mentors should avoid getting involved with their mentees.

■ **Bullying**

Bullying typically involves humiliation and threats as a way of emphasizing a power imbalance, engendering helplessness and psychological consequences in those who are targets. It probably occurs much more often than other, illegal actions, and it's difficult to prove. Unfortunately, when those who are bullied don't address the behavior directly and early, bullying tends to get worse.

■ **Unethical scholarly behavior**

Falsifying data, lying, forging documents, plagiarizing, or asking a mentee to publish or promote inaccurate findings hurts everyone involved in a project— and can tarnish the mentee's reputation. Perhaps more common, mentors sometimes take credit for a mentee's work or fail to credit their contributions (say, with appropriate authorship).

Inappropriate behavior outside the mentoring relationship

Protecting a mentee from harassment and mistreatment is one of a mentor's biggest responsibilities. Upon learning (from direct observation, from the mentee, or from someone else) about a mentee's mistreatment by a colleague, for example, the mentor might coach the mentee about addressing the colleague, speak to the colleague directly, notify department or university leaders, or even— if local authorities are unresponsive or uninterested—report the inappropriate behavior to outside organizations.

As optimists, we like to emphasize opportunities as well as challenges. Mentors are in a great position to promote a positive culture in which everyone's dignity is recognized and respected. Their influence can extend beyond the immediate research group, setting an example in their larger institution and modeling behavior for their mentees to remember when they become mentors. The table on the next page lists some ways that mentors can help their mentees directly and promote appropriate behavior broadly.

How can mentors promote appropriate behavior?

ACTION OR ATTITUDE	RATIONALE
Treat all mentees fairly	▪ Apply the same standards to all your mentees and be consistent in the way you behave with them. Don't favor some with better opportunities, more attention, or more encouraging feedback. ▪ It's natural to like or understand some mentees better than others, but don't let those preferences interfere with respectful, equitable treatment.
Set policies for appropriate behavior	▪ Policies are an opportunity to enact values and promote fair, decent treatment in the group. ▪ Mentors should talk about their policies with their mentees and general work group.
Respect mentees' preferences	▪ Each mentee is allowed to set more formal personal limits if they wish. ▪ Remember that mentees should have more say than mentors about levels of friendliness and privacy.
Create an atmosphere in which mentees feel safe	▪ Mentees deserve the freedom and safety to pursue their scientific and career goals. ▪ Give mentees the right to raise concerns without fear of retaliation or ridicule.
Promote an equal, inclusive culture in your lab or research group, department, and institution	▪ Mentors have the opportunity to create a healthy, productive, respectful environments on many levels. ▪ Mentors' actions in their own settings can contribute to a stronger larger atmosphere.
Lead your mentees by example	▪ Mentors set the tone for the group and inspire others to create a stronger, more respectful atmosphere. ▪ Mentees will become mentors someday, and this will help them behave professionally in those roles.
Provide training in professional behavior	▪ Career development includes learning to define and implement professional behavior. ▪ Explicit attention to professional, appropriate behavior is a valuable component of mentors' guidance.

What to do when inappropriate behavior occurs

The unfortunate reality is that bad behavior happens everywhere. Defining appropriate behavior and making a commitment to behave ethically will help mentors, mentees, and many others around them, but these aren't enough to stop people who don't understand social norms, choose to use their power selfishly, or can't obey the rules of human decency.

The system often seems to be on the side of power, but when misconduct occurs, those experiencing or witnessing it can find ways to deal with it effectively. Here are some possible steps that are useful for both mentors and mentees.

- **If you decide to address inappropriate behavior directly, have the conversation in public or with another person present.**
  The direct approach can sometimes be the best: naming the behavior, expressing your displeasure, and, with a witness, getting confirmation of what happened. If you take this route, describe the behavior briefly and tell the person clearly that you want them to stop. This doesn't always solve the problem (and with a serial or predatory person, it's unlikely to have much effect), but it can be an important first step. But if speaking to the offending person could make the problem worse, lead to retaliation, or endanger you in any way (including your emotional state), don't do it. Remember: the behavior is wrong whether or not you address the offender.

- **Discuss the experience with others in your workplace.**
  When something is wrong, you shouldn't keep it secret. If your mentor is not involved in the inappropriate behavior, inform them and ask their advice. Telling others about your experience can be helpful if an official investigation is necessary.

- **If inappropriate behavior does not end or interferes with your health or professional progress, consider reporting it.**

  Every university has a Title IX office that addresses sexual harassment and gender-based discrimination in its educational and employment settings. Members of the office should be able to help you understand and weigh the options for dealing with inappropriate behavior formally.

- **When you witness inappropriate or unprofessional behavior, speak up.**

  The behavior of bystanders is critical in changing improper practices and improving cultures. Calling out bad behavior can occur in many ways, from saying something spontaneous (such as "Wow" or "Wait, what did you just say?") to following formal channels. Seek guidance from a mentor or those with expertise on this issue if you are dealing with an egregious, longstanding, or pervasive form of unprofessional behavior.

- **Take care of yourself.**

  Experiencing inappropriate behavior takes a toll on mental health. Seek psychotherapy or pharmacologic treatment if you need it. In addition, get sleep, find time to exercise, and practice a form of relaxation. These actions will help you manage the stress of this experience and move forward strongly.

No one likes to discuss bad behavior, and some (too many, actually) would prefer even to think it doesn't exist. But it does. We can't ever eliminate it, but by honoring some clear guidelines in our own relationships and our own workplaces, we can make sure that inappropriate actions are limited—and promptly addressed.

Exercise 8 | How well do you foster ethical and professional behavior?

For Mentors

Check each item that fits your current mentoring experience or approach.

☐ It's my responsibility to maintain an ethical culture in my workplace.

☐ I set and observe limits and values about my behavior and self-control.

☐ In my position, I may receive very different treatment from colleagues or organizations than my mentees do, which can limit my perspective.

☐ When my mentees experience unfair, harassing, or discriminatory treatment, I am aware of it or want them to tell me.

☐ I try to be open to hearing my mentees' concerns about my behavior.

☐ I promote equal and respectful treatment among my mentees.

☐ I see myself as an ally and supporter, helping my mentees address improper behavior when they have experienced it.

☐ I can take steps to improve the professionalism and equality in my lab or research group.

☐ I am aware of the ways that unprofessional or inappropriate behavior can manifest in my workplace.

☐ I know how to address inappropriate behavior formally at my institution.

For Mentees

Check each item that fits your current mentoring experience or approach.

- [ ] My mentor understands the challenges I face when dealing with issues of fairness, professionalism, and appropriate behavior at my institution.

- [ ] I can discuss the definitions and limits of appropriate behavior with my mentor.

- [ ] Mentoring should include explicit discussion and modeling of appropriate behavior.

- [ ] I can ask my mentor for advice on my response to inappropriate or unprofessional behavior.

- [ ] I try to be aware of my biases, explicit or implicit.

- [ ] My mentor would give me guidance and support if I needed to take action after experiencing inappropriate behavior.

- [ ] I feel equipped to raise difficult or awkward issues about appropriate behavior in the mentoring relationship.

- [ ] In addition to my mentor, I can identify peers, other mentors, or other leaders who could provide casual or formal guidance about issues of professionalism.

- [ ] I know how to find and use my institution's resources for promoting fair and appropriate behavior.

- [ ] Through mentoring, I am acquiring skills for promoting appropriate behavior when I become a mentor.

CHAPTER 9
Embracing Change: Technology, Communication, & Generational Issues

A recent video call with collaborators in the eastern United States, the US West Coast, and Australia showed us that the only challenge to working together was our sleep schedules. This applies equally to mentoring, which today can be mediated through video conferencing, document-sharing, and real-time collaborative work. The many ways to write, revise, and sign documents all but magically transport us to other locations and have increased the ease and pace of work. Technology has changed everything.

In this chapter, we address three considerations in contemporary mentoring: technology, communication, and generational differences. Mentors and mentees usually come from different generations with different communication preferences and comfort levels. We know that not all members of one generation are alike, and we know that people don't usually spend much time considering how they use technology and prefer to communicate. But because these are the scaffolding for much of today's mentoring, we think they merit attention. In the era of remote mentoring during COVID, these issues have become especially pressing.

Opportunities today seem limitless. We have worlds of information available, with searches taking a fraction of a second. We can mentor more efficiently, sharing work nearly instantly. With texting or online messaging, questions can be answered and setbacks overcome in almost real time. We can expand our scholarly work into other topics, techniques, and fields by communicating with colleagues around the world, striking up new collaborations with ease. Mentoring itself is becoming more inclusive, with scholars in remote areas or poorly resourced institutions getting help from people in top-ranked universities and facilities in busy urban centers.

Case Example 17 | **Instant Messaging —But Not Instant Mentoring**

Melissa, a postdoctoral fellow at a university in the Midwest, is delighted to start a long-distance mentoring arrangement with Colleen, who has worked at a large research university in California for more than three decades. For their first meeting, scheduled for 11am Melissa's time, they agree to discuss a draft of a paper Melissa hopes to submit the following week. At 9am her time on the morning of the meeting, Melissa emails Colleen a link to a video meeting app and a draft of her paper. When they try to start their meeting, however, the app is glitchy, and they have to resort to texting until it gets going. Once they can see and hear each other, Melissa reels off a list of questions about her paper, which frustrates Colleen. When Colleen tells Melissa she isn't prepared to discuss the paper in detail, Melissa feels a little insulted.

For their next meeting, Melissa sends Colleen an invitation from another app, which requires both mentor and mentee to set up new accounts. Technology for that meeting proceeds smoothly. That's not the case for their next meeting, however: because Colleen expected to use the app from their first meeting and Melissa thought they'd be using the second app, their third conference starts 10 minutes late. Colleen had planned to review a section of a grant that Melissa had emailed the night before, but a work problem popped up, and she ran out of time. When they meet by video for a fourth time, Colleen raises two topics: their timeline for reviewing materials and their means of communication.

With these subjects out in the open, they make clear plans for the timing, technology, and contents for future meetings. Melissa promises to send materials for review at least two days before each call and to be specific about what feedback she'd like. They agree to use the second app from then on. Their relief is mutual—and almost palpable.

Case Example 18 |
Assertiveness or Entitlement?

Pete, a newly appointed assistant professor, is worried about not being able to present his work at an upcoming conference. In the interest of keeping the conference small and the quality of the research high, the society hosting the conference has a strict policy of allowing only members and their invited guests to attend. Pete is doubly concerned: he needs an invitation to the conference and an invitation for submitting an abstract for a presentation of his work, and the submission deadline is only two weeks away. There is one promising option: Pete is a fellow in a program for early-career scientists, one that usually includes courtesy invitations to this conference. The program directors are working to secure this year's invitations, but they haven't arrived yet.

Pete imagines the worst: the deadline for poster presentations passes with no invitation, and he misses a huge opportunity. Increasingly anxious, he decides to take direct action and sends an email to the manager overseeing the conference planning. "As a fellow in the program," he writes, "I would like to obtain my invitation as soon as possible." The manager, who has never heard of Pete, contacts the program's liaison to the organization and asks, with evident frustration, "Am I now taking orders from this person?"

The professional society has always been generous about extending invitations to fellows in the program, and the program leaders resent the extra work required to make sure the relationship remains cordial. They send the conference manager a long, apologetic email and hope for the best. At the same time, the program's directors wonder if Pete even understands basic etiquette. When one director tells Pete that his request might have come across as demanding and maybe even self-centered, Pete says he's sorry "if it caused any inconvenience" and explains that he felt pressured to get the invitation. The director sees this as an excuse rather than an apology and isn't sure Pete really comprehends what happened. Fortunately, the conference manager responds kindly to the directors' email, and thinking about her longstanding relationship with them, she drops the matter.

Younger people, such as Melissa in the Case Example, are often enthusiastic about adopting new approaches and using new apps, while those from older generations, like Colleen, might be a little less keen. Both Case Examples hint at what some deem the challenges of mentoring people from the Millennial generation, including different senses of urgency and etiquette. There is give and take between mentors' and mentees' generational cultures, as the world inevitably moves toward the mentee's generational beat. In his desperation, Pete went over the heads of the career program directors, offending them as well as the conference manager, and then was clueless about how his actions affected those around him—and tainted their view of him.

Technology's challenges highlight the importance of mentoring's all-important general guidelines, the ones we have been emphasizing throughout this book: understand the other person's temperament and style (and where they might clash with yours), consider the possibilities available, be clear about expectations and preferences, be respectful of everyone, establish plans about communication, and provide useful feedback.

 The tricky side of technology

We all know that technology has big benefits—and potentially big drawbacks. Video interactions between mentor and mentee can seem deceptively casual, for example, inviting overly familiar behavior or weak preparation. When communicating remotely, distraction is a frequent danger. Misunderstanding can easily occur because the quirks and glitches of video platforms create awkward, less-than-natural interactions. Thanks to COVID-era work demands, we've all become familiar with the special exhaustion that goes along with remote meetings. Nonetheless, the usual rules of professional etiquette should always apply, with each person greeting the other, making some small talk if appropriate, not interrupting, attending to the business at hand, honoring the clock, and ending with formal "thank you"s and reminders about the next meeting. All the same, each form of technology has its optimal use, based on the circumstances (e.g., video calls for establishing trust early in the mentoring relationship) and the task at hand (e.g., email for exchanging documents).

Various formats offer varying opportunities for communicating clearly. Choose your format based on factors such as the material or information you expect to share, the nature of your topic, the difficulty of describing your stance, and the intensity with which you expect your conversation partner to respond. If you're concerned that you might not be able to make your point fully—or worse, be perceived as hiding something—opt for the more transparent video-based option over written or voice-only options. The point is to try the options, learn how they suit you and various situations, and choose from there.

Video conferencing, with faces and voices, usually allows a more comprehensive picture, but it's also possible to convey emotions in a text message. If you're shy, trying to maintain privacy, or working from home in your pajamas, you might prefer the privacy afforded by email or online messaging. Yet another lesson we've learned from the COVID era is that a phone call can often convey social signals more effectively than a video meeting, with its risks of freezing, delays, discontinuous transmission, and single-speaker-only algorithms.

Sometimes you'll use email to keep a formal record or avoid being misunderstood. But sometimes not putting things in writing has advantages. In some contexts—for example, researchers discussing potential funding of grants with representatives of the funding organization—you might be wise to limit communication to voice. You can often get a point across more easily and efficiently in a quick phone call or text than in an email. And, of course, individual preferences apply. This could have generational sources, as we discuss below, with people over 60 often preferring phone calls to texting or written formats to spoken.

As Melissa in the Case Example learned, being able to share a document quickly doesn't guarantee that a mentor will provide instant feedback. And, as Colleen learned, expectations about collaboration in the age of plentiful technology can occur faster than we can—or sometimes want to—keep up.

Communication options: what are mentors' and mentees' responsibilities?

Mentors, who are traditionally (but not always) older than their mentees, can be one step (or more) behind their mentees in comfort with new technology. They can also be accustomed to a work culture in which communication processes are very different from today's standards. As a result, they have special responsibilities.

- **Develop a set of preferred technologies.**
  You can outline these to mentees at the beginning of your interactions and update them as new technologies and techniques emerge.

- **Embrace new apps, websites, or formats.**
  If you're not yet comfortable using them at work, try them out on your friends and family members. Get suggestions from relatives or colleagues.

- **Swallow your pride and ask your mentees to show you new ways to communicate.**
  They often have a new-favorite app or technique, and they're almost always happy to help you adopt it.

- **Use traditional formats if you think they have clear advantages.**
  These days a request to talk by phone is almost always a surprise, but sometimes it's more efficient and direct than other ways of connecting.

Mentees' knowledge about new technology brings responsibilities for them, too.

- **When introducing or helping with new technology, be respectful.**
  Anyone over 60 has gotten a condescending lecture on technology from a young colleague or IT expert ("But it's so easy!"), so you'll win points by being respectful, expecting to invest some time, and avoiding jargon.

- **Appreciate that newer isn't always better.**
  The competition for better, faster, and more appealing apps can be fun, but it can come with a certain snobbery. Sometimes existing apps are more useful.

■ **Don't use social media to air your grievances.**

This is a rule that applies to everything and everyone in your workplace, including your mentor. Posting your frustrations can cause problems today—and down the road, when prospective mentors and employers will be able to see that information.

Our recommendations for optimal communication strategies echo others that we've threaded throughout this book, all tied to staying aware of the other's as well as your own strengths and styles. They include: plan ahead; choose your format with care; decide in advance how and when you'll exchange, review, and discuss material; be mindful of individual preferences in setting expectations about response time; choose and stick with specific modes of communication (email? text? Zoom? the old-fashioned phone?) for brief exchanges as well as longer meetings; be consistent and responsive; and stay flexible, because things sometimes will be wonky. And circumstances and options will change. Our final suggestion for using technology? On occasion, don't. Meet in person when possible.

 ## Generational issues

Traditionally, mentors and mentees were from different generations, with mentors typically about as old as a mentee's parents. But times have changed. Because some people start graduate school after years in another career, mentees can be older than their mentors. Who's more advanced in years isn't the issue. What matters is that generational differences can create a kind of culture shock between mentors and mentees, adding extra opportunities for confusion and misunderstanding.

Stereotypes of generations abound, with lots of speculation in business and academic circles about how generational differences influence workplace culture. Baby Boomers, many people claim, value long hours, hard work, and clear professional etiquette and don't mind getting recognition only occasionally. They are supposedly uncomfortable with technology and slow to adopt new approaches. Millennials might value flexible hours with plenty of time to work remotely, shorter working hours to allow time for hobbies and personal interests (even if it means less pay or slower career advancement), and frequent praise and accolades. They are seen as loving technology and happily spending more time adopting new apps doing traditional work tasks. Baby Boomers might put up with tedious tasks as part of their work experience, while Millennials might have less tolerance, instead wishing for challenging, meaningful activities. Members of Generation X, meanwhile, are thought to be ambitious but cynical, feeling ignored or judged as part of a generation wedged between these two larger-than-life groups.

The Millennial generation, which the Pew Research Center defines as those born between 1981 and 1996, deserves some extra attention here, as the largest segment of the US work force and the majority of graduate students, postdoctoral fellows, and junior faculty. Millennials, the unflattering stereotype says, are demanding, fickle, self-important, impatient, quickly distracted, egalitarian to the point of missing the presence of hierarchy, and—that damning "e" word—entitled. To put things in context, we've compared the three main generations in today's workforce.

TABLE 9.	HOW FAMILIAR ARE YOU WITH GENERATIONAL FACTS AND STEREOTYPES?		
	BABY BOOMERS	GENERATION X	MILLENNIALS
Birth years	1946-1964	1965-1980	1981-1996
Work perspective	Loyal	Cynical	Idealistic
Work goal	Succeed on a traditional path	Pursue a worthwhile career	Have a meaningful impact
Learning style	Traditional lectures and coursework	Structure with the chance to think independently	Interactive, informal, group-based, or virtual formats
Work-life association	Adapt life to work	Strive for balance	Put work second to personal goals
Expectations about work role	Gradually climb the ladder to greater responsibility	Follow rules to advance	Quickly take on an influential role
Preference for feedback from mentors and supervisors	Formal supervision and guidance	Depth of collaboration, with meaning and structure	Frequent, detailed, feedback with ample praise
Technology stance	Interested but skeptical	Practical	Flexible, curious, enthusiastic
Preferred means of communication	In person or by phone	By email or video call	By any means: the more innovative, the better
Philosophy of communication	Formal style and mentor-driven format are most effective	Flexible is best, with format based on preferences	Should be informal and based on mentee's timeline
Perceived value of mentoring	Moderate. Part of formal activities.	High. Complements training and helps guide striving.	Limited. Temporary and not worth investing much effort.

As mentees, Millennials are supposedly so accustomed to encouragement and praise that they might appear inconsiderate or disrespectful. After all, if someone has received constant attention and accolades, any one mentor's support might seem pretty paltry. For some mentors, Millennials' bravado, self-assuredness, and belief that they should ask for what they want can look like demanding behavior.

Of course there's a strikingly positive side to the Millennials' culture. People in this generation hold strong convictions, want to make a difference in the world, are passionate about doing meaningful work, have the self-assurance to speak up, and aren't afraid to challenge conventions. Generally speaking, this group brings a refreshing attitude to the workplace. As mentees, they can help push scholarly work forward, contribute creativity and enthusiasm, and keep mentoring relationships genuine and honest.

Not all members of any one group are identical, and stereotypes are oversimplifications that can be hurtful. Mentors and mentees should be aware of generational styles but committed to understanding and responding to the identity and characteristics of each person.

 Mentoring Millennials

The unique technology savvy and communication preferences of this generation, combined with a culture that values growth and meaning, suggest that mentors stand to benefit by adapting to this group. Many of the mentoring techniques we discuss here, like so many mentioned throughout this book, will be helpful for mentees of any generation. If you're not sure what's important to your mentee (from any generation or background), ask.

Here are some general recommendations for mentoring Millennials.

■ **Provide frequent, informal feedback.**
  This generation values assessment of their performance. There's also no harm in asking each mentee, "How do you like to receive feedback?"

- ■ **Recognize their contributions with rewards.**
  In academia, this can mean nominating them for prizes or awards. It could also mean creating chances to publicly praise their achievements.

- ■ **Give them opportunities to learn and grow.**
  Millennials are often described as focused on doing meaningful work. They might like to jump right into the important projects and procedures in their workplaces.

- ■ **Show mentees how working with you will further their goals.**
  They want to know what they're getting for their hard work. You want to define how their activities will move them toward their scholarly and career goals.

In many ways, these are values and behaviors we've been promoting throughout this book. We believe in personalizing mentoring, creating an inclusive culture, promoting mentees' development, providing opportunities, and helping mentees become mentors. So maybe we, a Gen Xer and a Silent Generation member, are more Millennial-thinking than we realized. Maybe our progressive tendencies have led us to be influenced by the expectations and values of our younger colleagues and mentees. In any case, we believe that these practices aren't specific to any generation.

Because Millennials tend to be forthright, some business and academic experts have said that mentors should give them some training in workplace etiquette. This might include explicit communication about expectations, work schedules, and professional versus unprofessional behavior. We've seen mentees who don't seem to say "please" and "thank you," can't make polite chitchat, and appear unable to use openings, titles, and sign-offs in email messages. Instead of lamenting what can seem like self-centeredness or a lack of civility, why not tell those mentees what is expected during professional interactions and how specific communication styles might be perceived by people who are less familiar with them? Establish guidelines about polite behavior and keep mentees accountable to them, and you will then help them put these principles into practice. Model appropriate behavior and you will provide another avenue for learning.

Advice to Millennial mentees

- **Stay humble.**

  Getting credit and plum assignments for your talent can be great, but think about humility and hard work as another valuable path to achievement.

- **Plan to be independent.**

  In academia, organizations, institutions, and individuals value persistence in an atmosphere of infrequent accolades. That can feel a bit punishing, but it's good to earn your reputation and master approaches yourself.

- **Don't expect to change the entire culture.**

  No environment, including academia, is perfect. But spend some time learning how people interact and how tasks get done. Suggest innovations and show you care about improvement, but don't start out trying to heroically overhaul the system.

- **Show curiosity about your mentors' style and expectations.**

  It's better to approach differences with interest rather than a dismissive attitude. At the very least, doing so will flatter others and give you useful information.

Generation gaps and new technologies will always be with us, but with careful attention, mutual respect, and genuine interest, everyone can thrive in this brave new world. And perhaps more than any other, this is one arena in which mentees can be the teachers.

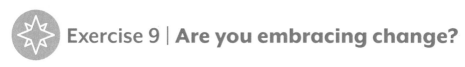

Exercise 9 | Are you embracing change?

For Mentors

Check each item that fits your current mentoring experience or approach.

☐ I like to improve my systems and procedures for mentoring.

☐ I enjoy using new apps and other new technologies when communicating with my mentees.

☐ Technology provides ways to enhance the mentoring relationship.

☐ New ways of working and communicating can help mentors to adapt to the needs, goals, and styles of their mentees.

☐ I take others' communication preferences into account when I make plans for meeting, reviewing documents, or sharing information.

☐ When I set the terms of mentoring with mentees, I make sure we identify the forms of technology we'll use for communication.

☐ Even though I try to establish a system for communicating with mentees, I am flexible about using several forms of communication.

☐ In the realm of technology and communication, I am aware of my preferences, frustrations, and comfort with change.

☐ I try to understand generational (and individual) differences in work style, values, and expectations in my mentees.

☐ I am able to give mentees feedback about workplace behaviors that might create difficulties for their success.

☐ I try to learn about and adapt to mentees' preferences for feedback and attention.

☐ I am aware of the areas in which I need to improve when dealing with technology, communication, and generational factors.

For Mentees

Check each item that fits your current mentoring experience or approach.

☐ I can speak directly with my mentor about my preferences for communicating, using technology, and getting feedback on my work.

☐ I enjoy helping my mentor identify and use new technologies that could improve the efficiency or communication of our mentoring.

☐ I am willing to negotiate with my mentor to determine a schedule for submitting my work and obtaining feedback.

☐ My mentor might not be accustomed to giving feedback on the schedule or in the style I prefer.

☐ I'm willing to compromise with my mentor about how we communicate.

☐ When joining a new lab or research group, I try to learn about the expectations around making requests and conveying opinions.

☐ I can adapt to the etiquette for appropriate behavior in my workplace.

☐ If I suggest improvements or updates at work, I try to take into account the existing culture.

☐ In some academic settings, frequent praise might not be the norm, but the culture can still support my progress.

☐ I am comfortable receiving feedback about professional behavior.

☐ I understand the differences (and varying consequences) between making requests and making demands.

☐ I am aware of the areas in which I need to improve when dealing with technology, communication, and generational factors.

Epilogue

We hope this book inspires and informs you.

Throughout these chapters we've aimed to explain our view that while mentoring can still happen in the traditional way, exciting new forms—long-distance, peer, short-term, and even speed mentoring—all offer opportunities and possibilities that are particularly well suited to today's fast pace, changing technology, and diverse world.

Whatever the form and however technology speeds things along, however, we believe that both mentors and mentees benefit most when they focus on some fundamental principles and ideals. The basics include commitment, self-awareness, tolerance, flexibility, enthusiasm, interest in another's perspective and progress, persistence, and clear communication. More sophisticated ones include respect for differences and interest in diversity, understanding of proper behavior, and openness to change and new technology.

You might find this surprising, but one reason we've written this book is that we believe mentoring isn't for everyone. Academia, business, and the nonprofit world might all seem to demand mentoring, but if this work isn't your forte, leave it to those who find it satisfying—if always challenging.

Our prescription for effective mentoring is a tall order, we know. But our experiences, in our own careers and through the Career Development Institute, have shown us that strong, effective mentoring is good for the mentee, the mentor, and the field in which they work. When you commit to mentoring effectively, the road ahead will undoubtedly have its bumps, but it will always be an interesting and rewarding two-way street.

As we noted at the start of this book, the COVID-19 crisis has changed everything: how we live, how we work, and how we communicate. Our future is uncertain, but we're confident about one thing: good mentoring helps scholars succeed. And successful scholars can find solutions that could be crucial for our long-term survival.

Lessons from the Career Development Institute

It started in the 1980s as a small program at the University of Pittsburgh, a weekly workshop designed to help and retain young scholars in the university's psychiatry department. A seminar for postdoctoral fellows in psychiatry, whether they held PhDs, MDs, or other doctoral degrees, it provided peer support, guidance from faculty members, and practical skills. The idea was to encourage junior scientists, introduce them to the university community, and give them the support and tools they needed to start their careers as researchers. It worked: many who arrived at Pitt as psychiatry residents, clinical psychology interns, or postdoctoral fellows stayed for years or decades, despite their original plan to spend a little time in Pittsburgh and then move on.

The program has expanded. The National Institute of Mental Health, taking note of Pitt's ability to retain young scientists, encouraged David to extend the model to other trainees across the United States, and in 2003 David and Alan Schatzberg, then chair of the Department of Psychiatry and Behavioral Sciences at Stanford University, established the Career Development Institute for Psychiatry (CDI). The program is aimed at a particularly vulnerable group: those who are finishing their research training or are very early in their first faculty appointments. It accepts applications from people in their final year of MD or PhD programs, advanced postdoctoral students, or junior faculty who have been working in their field less than two years. After serving as a CDI faculty member, Erika has taken on a leadership role, officially stepping in for David when he retired, and is now a CDI director.

In the past decades, more than 200 scientists from all around the United States have passed through the CDI, which is now a two-year program with formal activities, a support system that includes peers, CDI alumni, and faculty, and long-term mentoring. As far as we know, there's nothing like the CDI anywhere else in the world.

Our philosophy of mentoring has evolved with the CDI's own evolution. Shaped by new ideas, successes, and, of course, failures, we continue to strive for a model of mentoring that will serve the next generations of academics. We appreciate that not everyone who starts on the path to scientific independence will end up in a university, or even as a scientist. The same is true of scholars in the humanities, for whom faculty positions are even more difficult to obtain. We've incorporated technology and techniques from many fields and sectors into mentoring as it occurs in the CDI. We know that mentees grow into mentors and have worked to prepare them for that transition.

Along the way, we've developed some practices to make mentoring more useful. Commitment and confidentiality are essential. And we can't overestimate the value of planning. Often, negotiation is part of determining plans. Because we're scientists, we believe that evidence should guide what we do, so we collect data on mentors' performance, mentees' engagement, and the contents and quality of mentoring interactions.

The CDI has been our laboratory, an opportunity to test different approaches to mentoring. Through this program we've experimented with mentors' roles; the format, content, and timing of mentoring; and the cultivation of a larger mentoring culture. We've included 30-minute mentoring sessions, formalized a system of long-distance and long-term mentoring, and introduced peer mentoring. In its initial stages, David and Alan tried to mentor every fellow, a system that soon proved unworkable. Now, every CDI fellow is assigned a mentor from among the CDI's faculty, and the two have structured contact for at least two years. We match mentors and fellows carefully, with detailed advice from Leslie Dunn, the administrator of the CDI who conducts detailed interviews with each fellow at entry. This formal process has become a CDI capstone. We've sometimes heard complaints when we've matched a mentee to someone who isn't directly involved in the mentee's field, but once the two settle in, the complaints almost always disappear. Good mentoring, we find, can cross disciplines, ages, and even interests.

We've also had to reckon with our fellows' mentors back at their home institutions. Certain qualities matter for young researchers' success, and CDI faculty members sometimes end up coaching fellows on how to manage or even leave their local mentoring relationships when those qualities are missing. As we have noted, famous and fabulously successful scientists are not necessarily effective mentors. In addition to having its own value, CDI mentoring can provide an experience that's complementary to the fellows' ongoing mentoring experience.

We've become meta-mentors—or maybe mentor coaches—to provide the context for effective mentoring. Sometimes mentors need their own mentoring, and we consider that part of our mission. We now have a training session for CDI faculty mentors at every workshop.

A central part of the CDI experience is learning how to approach negotiations. David has the good fortune to be the father of an expert negotiator, Andrea Kupfer Schneider, and Andrea has led a negotiation training session at every CDI workshop since 2011. By providing a framework with an emphasis on self-knowledge, preparation, and skills, the session addresses critical academic concerns such as resources, relocation, and management. The bottom-line message: be flexible and persevere to get what you want.

As department chair for 26 years, David has experience on both sides of the negotiating table. He notes that if you can strive to understand what your chair, department, or organization wants—in other words, to think beyond what you'd like to achieve—you will have a powerful tool. It's also valuable to set a friendly, constructive tone. Rather than making things adversarial, you want the chair to be predisposed to help you. If you use empathy to understand the chair's position, maintain flexibility about your goals, and bring up concerns as issues that the two of you can solve together (not as demands or complaints) the chair will want to help. And don't forget to ask your mentor for advice and opportunities to practice before that negotiation.

What have learned from this laboratory?

One of our most valuable discoveries is that long-term, long-distance mentoring has powerful value. Our fellows enjoy meeting with the CDI directors, faculty, and local experts (none of whom is paid, by the way) at our annual workshops, but they report that having a long-distance mentor who gets to know them over two years and helps them address their goals and struggles during this formative time shapes their careers in impressive ways. These mentors, they note, are committed to their advancement but have no personal stake in issues such as whether they move to a new institution, submit an NIH grant in June or October, or switch to a different local mentor. This disinterested (but far from uninterested) perspective paradoxically often creates an unusually strong, valuable connection.

Not surprisingly, the most humbling and difficult part of directing the CDI is confronting the occasional ill-fated mentor-fellow pairing. Before we make any switches, we gather information from both sides, try to keep fellows involved in mentoring, and work with mentors to find solutions. Sometimes we reassign, and sometimes we are able to resolve differences. Addressing a dyad's bumpy mentoring journey gives our faculty, our fellows, and us an opportunity to improve professional skills and reap rewards.

We've also found that most academics benefit from having multiple mentors, people whose expertise and strengths can help with particular challenges at particular times. These might be primary mentors, individuals who help secure large grants, provide access to new techniques, and advise on big research projects. They can also be complementary mentors. Perhaps someone who's a great writing coach can critique a manuscript. Or an experienced scientist can connect with a young scholar at an annual meeting and make introductions to experienced, interested colleagues. They all add up to a large, multifaceted network of supporters.

Through the CDI Diversity Initiative, we've tried to educate ourselves on best practices in building diversity, inclusion, and equity among our fellows and faculty. In evaluating our progress, we've learned some lessons. Specifically, we've done pretty well, especially with gender diversity, but not well enough.

We changed our approach to recruiting potential applicants, using direct and personal communication rather than generic announcements. We try to create an open culture by making sure our faculty composition also reflects many different backgrounds and identities. When selecting fellows, we strive to be more explicit about evaluating achievement in the context of bias, discrimination, or disadvantage. And one of our current goals is to focus on some factors we haven't given adequate consideration in the past, including LGBTQ+ identity, childhood socioeconomic disadvantage, and disability.

The CDI has also confirmed what we've indicated throughout this book: changing times and changing technology have shown that new forms of communication can enhance mentoring, whether that's for peers who want to exchange information before an in-person meeting, a dyad who connect across many miles, or people who meet once face-to-face and want to build their relationship through video apps in months to come.

One of David's trademark sayings is "Change happens. Adapt to it." And the ways we've incorporated technology into the CDI reflect our enthusiasm for evolving. We've also added a session on professional behavior to our workshop, where it dovetails nicely with our longstanding session on research ethics. Now that our CDI classes are populated with fellows from the Millennial generation, a session on managing generational differences in communication, work style, and expectations will be the next one we add to our lineup. We're enthusiastic about adapting as our workplace culture and our fellows' needs change.

Through our efforts to support early-stage clinical scientists in the field of mental health, we've created an extraordinary community. In the CDI, we've seen mentees and mentors become collaborators, helped mentees become mentors, and learned how to identify and train mentors. We've gone from having our directors serve as informal mentors to everyone on the faculty being devoted to individual, long-term, structured mentoring. We've created ways for fellows to remain involved in the CDI after their formal two-year program ends. We hope that CDI fellows and alumni feel that they're part of a supportive, committed, valuable group. We feel that way, and we've had the bonus of getting to know many of the rising stars in our field and feeling proud when we watch them build their careers.

We've found that the benefits of this community last years. The happy hours and reunions we host at national scientific meetings bring together fellows from many different phases, demonstrating the longevity of the CDI's effects. We've been especially pleased to see that the benefits of the CDI community can feed forward to trainees' local institutions, helping them give and obtain useful mentoring, build local mentoring groups, and foster camaraderie in other settings. Our current goals are keep improving mentoring in the CDI, share what we know with others, and continue this thriving community.

The Career Development Institute's most valuable and long-lasting lesson might be the importance of community. Whenever CDI fellows and faculty meet, in Pittsburgh or in Palo Alto or at some conference, we're stuck by the cohesion and comfort that our fellows find in each other's company. They were all once young researchers together, and they've maintained those important, fundamental connections through promotions, accomplishments, setbacks, and moves across institutions or sectors, always helping each other. They're peer mentors in the best sense. They've created their own network, a cadre of colleagues they can call on to help deal with a host of real-world questions and challenges. But they also appreciate the value of finding and working respectfully with others—of all ages, in various places—who can help them deal with the challenges of academia. Wherever they are, they carry with them the idea that mentoring is essential to survival and success.

Resources

This list is hardly comprehensive, but it includes some books and articles that have helped us understand the challenges and joys of mentoring.

Chapter 1: What is Mentoring?

The Career Development Institute for Psychiatry: Co-located at the University of Pittsburgh and Stanford University, the CDI is dedicated to helping mental health researchers with launching and maintaining careers. www.cdi.pitt.edu

- Tips for starting as a principal investigator (PI): "The Surprises of Starting as a New PI" by Elisabeth Pain
  http://www.sciencemag.org/careers/2018/09/surprises-starting-new-pi

- Cultivating a positive lab environment: "Health Tips for Research Groups"
  https://www.nature.com/articles/d41586-018-05146-5

- The limits of networking: "Good News for Young Strivers: Networking is Overrated" by Adam Grant
  https://www.nytimes.com/2017/08/24/opinion/sunday/networking-connections-business.html

Some worthwhile books on mentoring, from the fundamental to the unconventional:

- On Being a Mentor: *A Guide for Higher Education Faculty by W. Brad Johnson*

- *Every Other Thursday: Stories and Strategies from Successful Women Scientists* by Ellen Daniell

- *The Mentor's Guide* by Lois J. Zachary

- *10 Steps to Successful Mentoring* by Wendy Axelrod

- *Mentors: How to Help and Be Helped* by Russell Brand

Chapter 2: The Mentoring Relationship

- Developing a plan for mentoring expectations: "Ten Simple Rules for Developing a Mentor–mentee Expectations Document" by Kristyn S. Masters and Pamela K. Kreeger
  https://journals.plos.org/ploscompbiol/article?id=10.1371/journal.pcbi.1005709

- First major story about the University of Rochester harassment case: "Amid Sexual Harassment Allegations, University of Rochester Grapples with Student Outrage" by Madison Pauly
  https://www.motherjones.com/politics/2017/09/amid-sexual-harassment-allegations-university-of-rochester-grapples-with-student-outrage/

- Sexual harassment case at the University of Rochester: "University of Rochester President Resigns as Outside Attorney Issues Report on Sexual Harassment Case" by Meredith Wadman
  https://www.sciencemag.org/news/2018/01/breaking-investigator-says-noted-linguist-accused-sexual-harassment-broke-no-laws-or

- Research paper with acknowledgment about postdoctoral fellow's suicide: "The Human Costs of the Pressures of Postdoctoral Research" by Pete Etchells
  https://www.theguardian.com/science/head-quarters/2017/aug/10/the-human-cost-of-the-pressures-of-postdoctoral-research

Chapter 3: What Makes an Effective Mentor?

- The National Research Mentoring Network
  https://nrmnet.net/

- Advice for improving mentoring: "Top 10 Tips to Maximize Your Mentoring" by Joan M. Lakoski
  http://www.sciencemag.org/careers/2009/08/top-10-tips-maximize-your-mentoring

- Nature's Guide for Mentors
  https://www.nature.com/articles/447791a

Chapter 4: Mentoring as a Classroom for Negotiation

- The Dynamic Negotiation Approach Diagnostic (DYNAD): Schneider, Andrea Kupfer and Gerarda Brown, Jennifer. Dynamic Negotiating Approach Diagnostic (DYNAD) (April 2, 2013). Marquette Law School Legal Studies Paper, No. 13-11.
  https://ssrn.com/abstract=2243679 or http://dx.doi.org/10.2139/ssrn.2243679

- David Kupfer's and Andrea Kupfer Schneider's book on negotiation: Schneider, Andrea & Kupfer, David. (2017). *Smart and Savvy: Negotiation Strategies in Academia.* Park City, UT: Meadows Press.

Chapter 5: Common Challenges in Mentoring

- Mentor evaluation forms
  https://ictr.wisc.edu/mentoring/mentor-evaluation-form-examples/

- Microaggression, a definition and examples: "Microaggressions: More than Just Race" by Derald Wing Sue
  https://www.psychologytoday.com/us/blog/microaggressions-in-everyday-life/201011/microaggressions-more-just-race

Chapter 6: Variations on a Theme: Long-Distance, Short-Term, Speed, & Peer Mentoring

- Resources and information about various forms of mentoring: The National Mentoring Resource Network
  https://nrmnet.net/nrmn-resources/

- Speed mentoring: "Speed Mentoring: Seven Steps to a Successful Session"
  https://edgeforscholars.org/speed-mentoring-seven-steps-to-a-successful-session/

- "Is 'Speed Mentoring' Really Mentoring?"
  https://artofmentoring.net/speed-mentoring/

- Peer Mentoring: "The Benefits of Peer Mentoring" by Carol Williams-Nickelson

  http://www.apa.org/gradpsych/2007/11/matters.aspx

  https://nationalmentoringresourcecenter.org/index.php/30-topic-areas/152-peer-mentoring.html

- Getting started: "40 Questions to Ask a Mentor" by Jo Miller

  https://www.forbes.com/sites/jomiller/2018/03/25/40-questions-to-ask-a-mentor/2/#3d55b1b37276

Chapter 7: Diversity & Mentoring

- *New York Times Magazine* article on women in science: "Why Are There Still So Few Women in Science?" by Eileen Pollack

  https://www.nytimes.com/2013/10/06/magazine/why-are-there-still-so-few-women-in-science.html

- National Institutes of Health Office of Scientific Workforce Diversity

  https://diversity.nih.gov/

- NIH Diversity Toolkit

  https://diversity.nih.gov/blog/2018-09-18-because-you-asked-more-information-about-nih-scientific-workforce-diversity-toolkit

- Research site with implicit association tests, to become familiar with your biases and attitudes about race, gender, sexual orientation, and other topics

  implicit.harvard.edu/implicit/takeatest.html

Suggestions for becoming informed and educated about racial equity and inclusion, with thanks to CDI alumna and faculty member Carolyn Rodriguez of Stanford University

- "How to Be an Anti-Racist" by Ibram Kendi

- "So You Want to Talk about Race" by Ijeoma Oluo

- Trevor Noah on the dominoes of racial injustice

  https://www.youtube.com/watch?v=v4amCfVbA_c

- A perspective on medical training from a white physician: "White Privilege in a White Coat: How Racism Shaped my Medical Education" by Max J. Romano

  https://www.annfammed.org/content/annalsfm/16/3/261.full.pdf

- Best Allyship Movement (BAM!) training modules from the University of Florida

  https://counseling.ufl.edu/resources/bam/

- "Beyond the Hashtag: How to Take Anti-Racist Action in Your Life," by Zyahna Bryant

  https://www.teenvogue.com/story/beyond-the-hashtag-how-to-take-anti-racist-action

- An example of group training programs to address racism

  https://www.pisab.org/

- Research by Dr. Lise Vesterlund and colleagues on improving and sustaining diversity in academia: "Gender Differences in Accepting and Receiving Requests for Tasks with Low Promotability," *American Economic Review*

  https://www.icos.umich.edu/sites/default/files/lecturereadinglists/03-A20141734-10703.pdf

- "Why Women Volunteer for Tasks that Don't Lead to Promotion" by Linda Babcock, Maria P. Recalde, and Lise Vesterlund

  https://hbr.org/2018/07/why-women-volunteer-for-tasks-that-dont-lead-to-promotions

- "How Costly is Diversity? Affirmative Action in Light of Gender Differences in Competitiveness" by Muriel Niederle, Carmit Segal, and Lise Vesterlund

  https://web.stanford.edu/~niederle/AAPaper.pdf

- Harvard Kennedy School Women and Public Policy Program, Gender Action Portal

  https://gap.hks.harvard.edu/

- NIH Director Francis Collins's decision to refuse Invitations for "manels": "NIH Director: No More 'Manels,' How To Make Panels More

Diverse" by Bruce Y. Lee
https://www.forbes.com/sites/brucelee/2019/06/15/nih-director-no-more-manels-how-to-make-panels-more-diverse/#490edce920d6

- A study of perceptions and experiences of gender bias among physicians: "Association of Physician Characteristics with Perceptions and Experiences of Gender Equity in an Academic Internal Medicine Department" by Shannon M. Ruzycki, Georgina Freeman, Aleem Bharwani, and Allison Brown
https://jamanetwork.com/journals/jamanetworkopen/fullarticle/2755310

Chapter 8: Professional Behavior

- Men mentoring women: "When Men Mentor Women"
https://hbr.org/podcast/2018/10/when-men-mentor-women

- Guidelines: "7 Essential Guidelines for Mentoring in the Post-Weinstein Era" by Kathy Gurchiek
https://www.shrm.org/resourcesandtools/hr-topics/behavioral-competencies/pages/guidelines-for-mentoring-in-the-postweinstein-era.aspx

Mentoring and harassment examples

- "University of Rochester and plaintiffs settle sexual harassment lawsuit for $9.4 million" by Meredith Wadman
https://www.sciencemag.org/news/2020/03/university-rochester-and-plaintiffs-settle-sexual-harassment-lawsuit-94-million#

- "Dartmouth College Professors Investigated Over Sexual Misconduct Allegations" by Katharine Q. Seelye and Stephanie Saul
https://www.nytimes.com/2017/10/31/us/dartmouth-professors-sexual-misconduct.html?smid=tw-nytimes&smtyp=cur

- "The Dartmouth Sexual Harassment Allegations are So Much Worse than I Thought" by Daniel Engber
  https://slate.com/technology/2018/11/dartmouth-sexual-assault-harassment-lawsuit-psychology.html

- "Dartmouth Reaches $14 Million Settlement in Sexual Abuse Lawsuit" by Anemona Hartocollis
  https://www.nytimes.com/2019/08/06/us/dartmouth-sexual-abuse-settlement.html

- "Women Speak Out about Former Northwestern Professor Alec Klein's Alleged Sexual Harassment" by Brittney McNamara
  https://www.teenvogue.com/story/northwestern-professor-alec-klein-alleged-sexual-harassment

- "The Dangerous Intimacy of Grad School: Was the N.Y.U. Harassment Case Inevitable?" by Ginia Bellafante
  https://www.nytimes.com/2018/08/18/nyregion/avitall-ronell-nyu-title-ix.html

- The difficulties of experiencing and reporting sexual harassment: "What Reporting Sexual Harassment Taught Me" by Simine Vazire
  https://slate.com/technology/2018/07/what-reporting-sexual-harassment-taught-me.html

- "How I Learned to Look Believable" by Eva Hagberg Fisher
  https://www.nytimes.com/interactive/2018/01/03/style/dressing-for-sexual-harassment-hearings.html

- Themes of mentor mistreatment of trainees in academia: "Are We in a Mentoring Crisis?"
  https://edgeforscholars.org/are-we-in-a-mentoring-crisis/

- Gender bias in an academic medicine department: "Association of Physician Characteristics With Perceptions and Experiences of Gender Equity in an Academic Internal Medicine Department"
  https://jamanetwork.com/journals/jamanetworkopen/fullarticle/2755310

Chapter 9: Embracing Change: Technology, Communication, & Generational Considerations

- The Pew Research Center's definitions of generations
  https://www.pewresearch.org/fact-tank/2019/01/17/where-millennials-end-and-generation-z-begins/

- The Millennial generation and the workplace: "How to Make Your Workplace Millennial Friendly" by Ashira Prossack
  https://www.forbes.com/sites/ashiraprossack1/2018/07/29/how-to-make-your-workplace-millennial-friendly/#3440d03e409d

- "What Do Millennials Really Want at Work? The Same Things the Rest of Us Do" by Bruce N. Pfau
  https://hbr.org/2016/04/what-do-millennials-really-want-at-work?utm_campaign=HBR&utm_source=linkedin&utm_medium=social

- A JAMA opinion piece for training medical researchers: "Mentoring Millennials" by Jennifer Waljee, Vineet Chopra, and Sanjay Saint
  https://jamanetwork.com/journals/jama/fullarticle/2765430?guestAccessKey=857000a4-d105-4293-b180-c4b334ce5642&utm_content=weekly_highlights&utm_term=051720&utm_source=silverchair&utm_campaign=jama_network&cmp=1&utm_medium=email

- "The Challenges and Opportunities of Teaching "Generation Y" by Jodie Eckleberry-Hunt and Jennifer Tucciarone
  https://www.ncbi.nlm.nih.gov/pmc/articles/PMC3244307/

- "7 Ways Millennials Can Transition Smoothly in a New Workplace" by Jayson DeMers
  https://www.inc.com/jayson-demers/7-ways-millennials-can-transition-smoothly-in-a-new-workplace.html

- "Key Statistics About Millennials in the Workplace"
  https://dynamicsignal.com/2018/10/09/key-statistics-millennials-in-the-workplace/

Dynamic Negotiating Approach Diagnostic (DYNAD) / Scoring Guide & Interpretation

Scoring the Instrument

When you are finished, transfer the number from each item on the tally sheet. For example, on item A, if you selected number 6, write "6" on the line designated for item A on the tally sheet. Then add the numbers.

SAMPLE: B 1 + H 4 = 5

Interpretation of the Instrument

1   This instrument gives you two sets of scores. Calm scores apply to your response to conflict when disagreement first arises. Storm scores apply to your response if things are not easily resolved and emotions and feelings of conflict get stronger.

2   The scores indicate your *preference*, or inclination to use each style. The higher your score in a given style, the more likely you are to use this style in responding to conflict. You can develop skills in the appropriate use of each conflict management style and, as such, are not limited to using the style(s) that you prefer.

Conflict Management Style Preferences - Tally Sheet

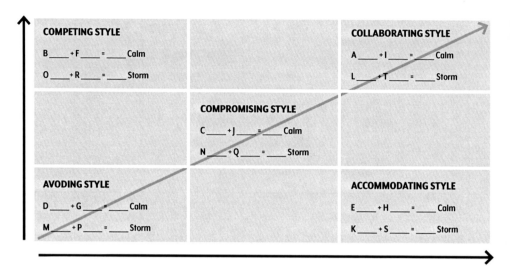

COMPETING STYLE

B ____ + F ____ = ____ Calm

O ____ + R ____ = ____ Storm

COLLABORATING STYLE

A ____ + I ____ = ____ Calm

L ____ + T ____ = ____ Storm

COMPROMISING STYLE

C ____ + J ____ = ____ Calm

N ____ + Q ____ = ____ Storm

AVODING STYLE

D ____ + G ____ = ____ Calm

M ____ + P ____ = ____ Storm

ACCOMMODATING STYLE

E ____ + H ____ = ____ Calm

K ____ + S ____ = ____ Storm

LEGEND (Arrows read low to high)

Vertical Arrow: ASSERTIVENESS: Getting your own needs met

Horizontal Arrow: EMPATHY: Maintaining the relationship between yourself and the other party

Diagonal Arrow: The relative amount of effort and creativity needed to use conflict management style

Style Advantages & Disadvantages

Competing

High Assertiveness/Low Empathy
"We're doing it my way ..."

Advantages

- Speed
- Decisiveness
- Preservation of Important Values
- Clarity

Disadvantages

- Harmed Relationships
- Loss of Cooperation
- Lack of Input or Feedback from Others

Best to Use in These Contexts

- When Need Quick Decision
- When in Charge and Expected or Needed
- When Key Values at Stake

Best to Use With These Counterparts

- With Accommodating to Get What You Want
- With Competing to Defend Yourself

Accommodating

Low Assertiveness/High Empathy
"OK, whatever you say ..."

Advantages

- Maintains Appreciation from Others
- Freedom From Hassle and Conflict (at Least in the Short Run)
- Defers to Others

Disadvantages

- Don't Get What You Want
- Frustration for Others Who Wish to Collaborate
- Loss of Respect From Others
- Denies Others Benefit of Healthy Confrontation

Best to Use in These Contexts

- When Issue is Not That Important
- When Relationship is Primary Interest

Best to Use With These Counterparts

- When Others' Interests are Primary
- When You Can "Bank" Accommodating
- With Other Accommodating Styles

Avoiding

Low Assertiveness/Low Empathy
"Let's not make a big deal out of this ..."

Advantages

- Keep Your Focus on Other Interests
- Freedom From Entanglement in Trivial Issues or Insignificant Relationships
- Preservation of Status Quo

Disadvantages

- Periodic Explosions of Pent-up Anger (from you or at you)
- Residue of Negative Feelings
- Stagnation
- Loss of Accountability or Participation
- Does Not Build Relationship

Best to Use in These Contexts

- When Your Interests are Unimportant
- When You Don't Have Energy or Focus to Negotiate
- When You are Unprepared to Negotiate

Best to Use With These Counterparts

- With Competing to Negotiate Over the Rules
- When Not Engaging will Allow Others to Negotiate to Lead
- When Others Will Solve

Compromising

Medium Assertiveness/Medium Empathy
"Let's find some middle ground ..."

Advantages

- Readily Understood by Most People
- Provides a Way Out of Stalemate
- Builds Atmosphere of Reasonableness Relatively Fast

Disadvantages

- Possibly Unprincipled Agreement
- Likelihood of Patching Symptoms and Ignoring Causes
- Can Be Mediocre and Unsatisfying to All

Best to Use in These Contexts

- At the End of the Dispute to Bridge a Gap
- To Help Shift Styles at the End

Best to Use With These Counterparts

- To Move a Competing Style to Trading Off
- With Other Compromising
- With Accommodating to Give Them Something

Collaborating

High Assertiveness/High Empathy

"My preference is ... I'm also interested in your views."

Advantages

- Builds Trust in Relationships
- High Cooperation & Compliance
- Merges Perspectives
- High Energy

Disadvantages

- Time Consuming
- Distraction From Other More Important Tasks
- Analysis Paralysis

Best to Use in These Contexts

- When Buy-in is Key to Compliance
- When Need Lots of Ideas
- When Want Team Building
- When Creative or Innovative Solution is Needed

Best to Use With These Counterparts

- With Other Collaborators
- With Competing to Move Them to Problem Solving
- With Compromising to Move Them To be More Creative

Acknowledgments

Many mentors, mentees, and colleagues made this book possible. We are grateful to all of them. Our own long-term mentoring experience has been the foundation of our collaboration on this book (and has led to some worthwhile science, too).

Much of this book was inspired by our experiences in the Career Development Institute for Psychiatry (CDI). Our co-director, Alan Schatzberg, has shaped our philosophy of mentoring and has modeled the commitment, wisdom, and caring of an expert mentor. We've also learned from the over 200 alumni of the CDI. They've given us the privilege of guiding them and have guided us in understanding the needs of early-stage mental health researchers. Many of those alumni are now faculty and the inspiration for some of the names used in our case examples. They've brought enthusiasm creativity, and innovation to our mission.

Paul Appelbaum, Ayana Jordan (CDI class of 2016), and Mark Matthews kindly read drafts and shared their wisdom on the best approaches to contemporary mentoring challenges. Ellen Frank, ace mentor and accomplished writer, helped us find clarity and focus. Amanda Trujillo kept us on track with many details.

Louisa Williams edited and re-edited to help us find a practical, punchy expression of our ideas in our own voices. Todd Germann used his creative powers to develop our ideas for a color scheme and title into a sophisticated design theme.

We thank the numerous mentees and mentors who've provided us with a deeply rewarding two-way experience in science, work relationships, and life.

Finally, we thank our families. Their curiosity, patience, and support made this a stronger book.

Made in United States
North Haven, CT
09 March 2022

16949325R00082